VerAegis

Contribution:

Live beyond Your Comfort Zone

~~Touch~~ Live a Life

~~Inspire~~ Make a Contribution

~~Ignite~~ Kindle a Spirit

James M. Haden

The Legacy Series

Books by James M. Haden

The Legacy Series:
VerAegis—Relationships
VerAegis—Contribution
VerAegis—Spirit

ISBN-10: **1512286672**
ISBN 13: **978-1512286670**

Dedication

I dedicate *VerAegis* to my wife, Sheri; my daughter, Teagan; and my son, Jimmy, whom I love and cherish deeply.

To all who read *VerAegis*:

In the Legacy Series, I've tried to capture many thoughts and cover some deep topics while keeping it simple and fun. This book series is designed to be an entertaining and informative reference for all aspects of everyday life. I hope that you are stimulated and challenged by *VerAegis—Contribution* and will find something of use and perhaps even life changing between its covers.

If you can't explain it simply, you don't understand it well enough.
Albert Einstein

Words are, of course, the most powerful drug used by mankind.
Rudyard Kipling

Table of Contents

Table of Figures

Introduction

It's all about quality of life and finding a happy balance between work and friends and family.

Sir Philip Green

The greatest obstacle to discovery is not ignorance—it is the illusion of knowledge.

Daniel J. Boorstin

I believe that being successful means having a balance of success stories across the many areas of your life. You can't truly be considered successful in your business life if your home life is in shambles.

Zig Ziglar

It isn't until you come to a spiritual understanding of who you are—not necessarily a religious feeling, but deep down, the spirit within—that you can begin to take control.

Oprah Winfrey

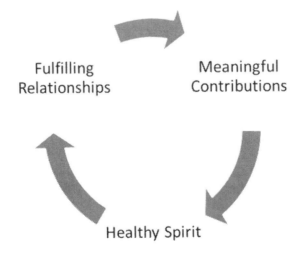

Fulfilling
Relationships

Meaningful
Contributions

Healthy Spirit

I have learned that age is necessary but not sufficient for gaining wisdom. Throughout my formative years of elementary and high school, many (if not all) of my teachers and coaches stressed that not only should I alone be an optimist but we should all view a partially filled glass as half-full rather than half-empty. At that time in my life, I reasoned that both views were (for all intents and purposes) equivalent and that my paradigm du jour would depend largely on my fondness for the liquid therein contained: was it a struggle to finish the task at hand, or did I savor every last sip, enjoying the challenge and potential reward?

Later in life, I read Jim Collins's book *Good to Great* and learned of the so-called Stockdale paradox. Collins described Admiral Jim Stockdale's tale of imprisonment and torture at the "Hanoi Hilton," a Vietnam prisoner-of-war camp. Stockdale was tortured over twenty times during his eight years of imprisonment from 1965 to 1973. As a prisoner, he had neither rights nor any idea of when he would be released. Yet he survived the horrific ordeal. Stockdale explained to Collins that the optimists didn't make it; they simply died of broken hearts as their expectations (based on unfounded hopes) were repeatedly dashed. They thought, "We'll be out by Christmas...Easter...summer," and each letdown killed part of their hearts until they eventually succumbed to despair. Stockdale went on to explain a profoundly important lesson about those who prevailed: "You must never confuse faith that you will prevail in the end—which you can never afford to lose—with the discipline to confront the most brutal facts of your current reality, whatever they might be (2001)."

I imagine the pessimists died next, as they did not have faith that they would prevail, and without hope, they had nothing to live for. Who was left? I like to refer to the survivors as pragmatic optimists. Jim Collins refers to the survivor phenomenon as the Stockdale paradox. Survivors are those who:

- are willing to face and deal with the reality of their situation, however dismal (pragmatic in attitude and action);

- are confident that they will prevail (retain an optimistic attitude); and
- do not set arbitrary goals based on false hopes (balance optimism with an equally pragmatic attitude).

Brian Dyson, former CEO of Coca-Cola from 1986 to 1991, delivered a memorable and inspirational speech to his many employees. In the speech, Dyson addressed a reality of life: we each have a great deal to balance, but when we approach our opportunities and problems in a healthy manner, we can prevail. To a great extent, I believe this speech is a reflection of Dyson's pragmatic optimism. My daughter, Teagan, was a newborn when a friend e-mailed a copy of Mr. Dyson's speech to me. At the time, I was working twelve to sixteen hours a day and trying to keep up with an increasing workload. Teagan was asleep when I left for work and, more often than not, asleep when I returned home. I read and reread this short, simple, yet powerful speech.

> Imagine life as a game in which you are juggling some five balls in the air. You name them—*work*, *family*, *health*, *friends*, and *spirit*...and you're keeping all of these in the air.
>
> You will soon understand that *work* is a rubber ball. If you drop it, it will bounce back. But the other four balls—*family*, *health*, *friends*, and *spirit*—are made of glass. If you drop one of these, they will be irrevocably scuffed, marked, nicked, damaged, or even shattered. They will never be the same. You must understand that and strive for it...Work efficiently during office hours and leave on time. Give proper time to your family and friends, and have proper rest. Value has a value only if its value is valued.

I lived and worked in Silicon Valley. My twenty-mile commute was so congested that I rode my bike two to four times a week to avoid traffic—and to take advantage of the opportunity to exercise. Riding 80 to 160 miles per week kept me in pretty good physical condition, but I was unable to sit for much more than ninety minutes without suffering shooting pain down my back and the side of my right leg. I walked to the office of a mentor and told him of my predicament. No matter what hours I worked, I could not keep up. "What should I do?" I asked. He smiled wryly and replied that when work becomes overwhelming, the only thing you can do is work more!

There I stood, with two pagers (one for general purposes–the other for emergency response) and a cell phone, feeling like roadkill on the information highway. I was in complete shock; the only advice he gave was to work more. I quietly left his office and mentally fired him as a mentor. On the way back to my office, I noticed a flyer advertising a lunchtime stress-management seminar scheduled for noon the next day. I cleared my calendar.

The next morning at eleven thirty, I snuck into the lunchroom, grabbed my sack lunch, and stealthily made my way into the conference room to await the seminar. Fifteen minutes later, the door opened. The presenter walked in, turned on the light, and was surprised to find me eating in the dark. She was taken aback when I explained that I had to be stealthy in order to avoid being pulled into some sort of crisis-management situation. I paraphrased Brian's speech to her and explained my situation. We spoke for a few minutes longer, until she had to set up for the class. As she prepared, I thought about our conversation in relation to Dyson's simple speech, and a powerful concept emerged: the consequences of stress are varied, but one thing is certain—as long as your actions are not aligned with your beliefs and values, you will remain stressed.

Considering the concept—aligning actions to values and beliefs—in conjunction with Brian Dyson's speech—and assuming that we truly believe that there is more to life than work, we must conclude that we need to allocate ample time to nurture (juggle) the glass balls in order to avoid undue stress. This stress will manifest itself in one or more of many symptoms, including anxiety, anger, aches, pains, and even illnesses. Once stress manifests itself as physical and emotional ailments, it is likely that we have already dropped the health ball, with the family, friends, and spirit balls not far behind.

The seminar concluded, and I left at one o'clock sharp. I called my wife, Sheri, and asked what time she was planned to have dinner. After she picked herself up from the floor (only a slight exaggeration of her surprise), we agreed to begin having family dinners each night at six thirty; I would call in advance if for some reason I could not make it on time. Within two weeks of eating together as a family, my back and leg pains were gone. I was in better spirits. I felt better, both physically and mentally. My family was happy, and (believe it or not) things got better at work—not worse.

In life, we are faced time and again with challenging circumstances, situations, and people who tend to pull us away from our intended paths. Yet we are defined not by these problems but by our responses to them. As Jesus stated over two thousand years ago, "If a house is divided against itself, that house cannot stand" (Mark 3:25 [NIV]). It follows that if our actions are "divided" against our beliefs, we "cannot stand"; the stress will take its toll. The solution is that when negatively (or even positively) motivated, we must choose to respond with an approach in line with our beliefs and values.

Upon further consideration of Brian Dyson's speech, we find that the balls we juggle fall into three primary sectors of our lives:

- Relationships: Family, friends, coworkers, mentors, and so on
- Contribution: Work, or what we give back
- Spirit: Spiritual and physical well-being. Are you in good spirits or ill-tempered and in poor spirits?

Essentially, the key to our effectiveness and ultimately our happiness is responding to life in a manner that balances relationships, contribution, and spirit. Note that spiritual and physical health are combined into the single category of spirit. This was done purposefully, because while physical health may falter and eventually fail, your spirit need not. I believe the combined message is that we need to be pragmatically optimistic that despite living in a chaotic world of information overload, we not only can focus our efforts on—but have the responsibility to focus on that which is important—not only on what is fun or urgent. Furthermore, the ability to focus; to direct the majority of our effort toward our highest priorities, is vital to our effectiveness.

Visualize life as a three-legged stool. One leg represents the health of your relationships, the next the impact of your contributions (negative or positive), and the final the health of your spirit. If one leg is short, the stool (your life) is wobbly and unstable. With two short legs, it is terribly wobbly and will possibly topple or collapse. Only with three solid legs will the stool effectively support the weight of its burden (Figure 1).

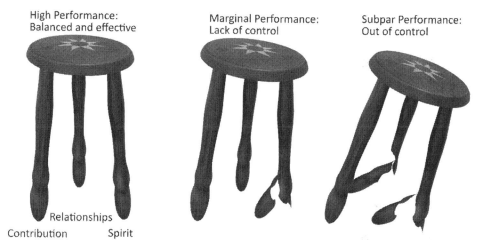

High Performance:
Balanced and effective

Marginal Performance:
Lack of control

Subpar Performance:
Out of control

Relationships
Contribution   Spirit

Figure 1: Being balanced and effective is possible only with three strong legs. Our relationships, sense of contribution, and spirits all must be healthy in order to achieve lasting effectiveness.

Accordingly, this series is organized into three books. Each book is represented by one leg of the stool:

- Relationships: Live your life. Touch another.
- Contribution: Make a difference. Inspire another.
- Spirit: Kindle your spirit. Ignite another.

A common thread links each of these three books: you *will* leave a legacy. It is within your power and responsibility to leave the legacy you desire.

Why *VerAegis*? Being VerAegis (Vĕr-ā-jis) represents a way of life that leads to balance between our contributions, our relationships, and the manner in which we approach life—our spirt. With balance comes the ability to significantly expand our comfort zones and be the authors of our legacies. Being VerAegis is daring to stretch beyond our current comfort zones.

Book 1 is devoted to relationships. Humans are social beings who rely on one another—not solely for survival but to derive the most from ourselves and from life. We will learn how to better manage our closest relationships while pondering the meanings of maturity, trust, and setting appropriate boundaries based on convictions and principles. We will consider reconciliation and the importance of family. We will dig into the fundamentals of thought and how to best manage change rather than becoming roadkill on the information highway. Most of all, we will enjoy our journey together.

Book 2 is devoted to our contribution—our ability to positively impact others. We often define ourselves by what we do, the impact we create, and the lives we affect. Not many people reach the end of their days lamenting that they should have worked more; in Book 2, we will dig into tools and techniques to help us to work smarter and learn how to better manage our finances and our time. We will learn how to set boundaries that allow us the freedom to think creatively about our contributions while balancing our time so that we do not neglect relationships or ourselves. We will dig more deeply into the applications of the fundamentals of thought and how to apply what we learned in Book 1. We will also expand the concept of change management and show how this simple model can be used to manage both innovation and continuous improvement. Finally we will investigate how to dream of a better us—a better future—and then how to set goals and make better decisions so that we can each reach those dreams.

Book 3 is devoted to our spirit—our ability to positively influence others. We are often judged by how we achieve our accomplishments;

how we impact the lives of those with whom we interact. We need to learn to set boundaries on how we relate to others as we manage our relationships and our contribution. Not many people reach the end of their days lamenting that they were loved by too many—or loved too many people. In Book 3, we will dig into how the choices we make affect our spirits and how our spirits influence our closest relationships. We will learn how to recognize and turn away from temptations and how to help others do so as well. We dig more deeply into principles and values and discuss in more detail the need to balance courage with consideration. We will learn about the purpose of anger and how to better manage our frustrations. We will ponder the golden rule, and we will learn of the need to call upon a higher authority to genuinely achieve our full potential. We will learn of parables and true stories of life. We will consider the legacies of well-known public figures whose values became misaligned with principles. Finally we will investigate how to invoke self-discipline and tap into an infinite source of power to better ourselves. We will learn to leverage the nature of our spirits to increase the value of our relationships and our contributions. We will learn to live beyond our comfort zones.

VerAegis Book 2: Contribution Is Fundamental to Your Well-Being

Make a difference in a manner that inspires others to emulate you. What better way to forge a legacy?

Whatever you are, be a good one.

Abraham Lincoln

You cannot escape the responsibility of tomorrow by evading it today.

Abraham Lincoln

For we are God's handiwork, created in Christ Jesus to do good works, which God prepared in advance for us to do.

Ephesians 2:10 (NIV)

You have to decide what your highest priorities are and have the courage (pleasantly, smilingly, non-apologetically) to say "no" to other things. And the way you do that is to have a bigger "yes" burning inside.

Stephen Covey

Will your burning yes be the drive to leave a legacy through your contribution?

From fifty thousand feet high, whether you are contributing to a family, a sports team, a business, or any other team—or simply leading your life—the activities required to be effective are strikingly similar. Effectiveness in all arenas requires the integrity to set and act on your priorities in such a way that you obtain your desired results time and time again.

Begin by imagining what you (or your team) want to become and what you desire the future to hold. Some (surprisingly few) people don't need plans or goals to be continuously effective over the long term; the rest of us require a systematic process to continually achieve our desired results.

Whether motivated to move from point A to point B, to create intimate relationships, to be at peace with self and others, or to live life to the fullest, enjoying every minute, create a vision of your desired future. Next, pragmatically define where you are today, noting the gaps between your present situation and your vision—your ideal future. Work with your team to quantify the gaps (if this is a personal vision, you may choose to work alone or with family and friends). Identify which gaps are easiest to fill and which gaps, when filled, will yield the greatest benefit. Create goals. Prioritize. Create more detailed plans for the highest priorities. Determine if you and your team are capable of executing the plans. If so, execute. If not, prepare, train, and then execute. Finally, model the behavior you would like others to follow, and evaluate your progress going forward, making adjustments as necessary (Figure 2).

This outline for change may seem simplistic (perhaps it is), but it is not easy. Even if you are planning to change only yourself, you will face trials and tribulations. If you add the dynamics of team members, organizational "memory" (the tendency for teams and organizations to get into "a groove" and stay there) and all the associated biases, the obstacles to change may appear insurmountable. But if your vision is

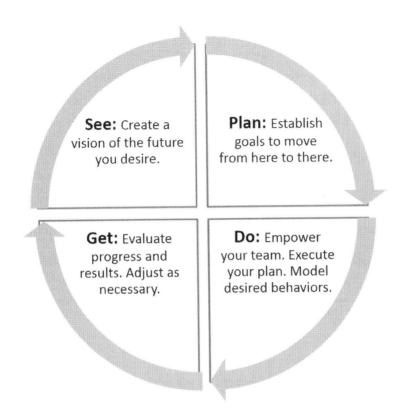

Figure 2: See-plan-do-get cycle for achieving a vision

worth achieving, you will persevere forging a path to success. While on this journey, remember that you are responsible for and can control your own actions and responses, but you can only influence the actions of others—and the strongest influence you have is modeling the behavior you desire from others.

Consider the following two sentences in the context of your contribution:

1. "I am doing well."
2. "I am doing good."

The first implies that you are good at what you do. You are competent and have skills. Others have faith that when you set out to achieve your goal, it will be done well.

The second implies the job you perform is a good deed or act. The goal you have set out to achieve is of good and noble intent. Your contribution is helping others, creating jobs, healing, creating smiles, making others feel secure, and spreading faith, hope, or joy. Your contribution matters to others and in some way connects with their core motivation to get things done, to create intimate relationships, to be at peace with yourself and others, or to live life to the fullest.

Relationships matter to your effectiveness, and your contributions affect your relationships. So it follows that doing good deeds in your daily life will further strengthen your relationships, increasing your circle of influence and subsequently your ability to contribute. People know when you are genuinely motivated to help others. Your motivation is a strong influence on your ability to influence others and, thus, your ability to make a positive difference. Some of us are born with the motivation to relate strongly to others; some people with a calm presence and ability to create peace and tranquility; others with the skill and motivation to create excitement; and still others with a keen ability to achieve. Regardless of your natural gifts, we learned in Book 1 of this Legacy Series that relationships are vital to our individual contribution and success.

The specific contribution you choose depends on your circumstances and relationships, but whatever it is, it doesn't require that you add more to your already full plate. For example, if you are juggling a career and a family, you do not need to volunteer at a charity in order to do "good works," but you do need to do good deeds during your workday and for your family and friends. For those of you who have time to volunteer without neglecting your other responsibilities and damaging your personal relationships, please do so. Your contribution is the sum of everything you do. Good deeds minus bad deeds equals your net contribution.

This is not a linear equation, however. One bad deed can overcome the effects of tens, hundreds, even thousands of good deeds. The tools in this section are designed to help you do good things well. The choice of which good things to do and how to do them belongs to you. Keep in mind that how we go about our good deeds must be aligned with solid principles; the ends do not justify the means. Doing a good deed in a bad way is not a positive net contribution. As we addressed in *VerAegis—Relationships*, to be effective, we must obtain good results in a manner that enables a repeat performance and that strengthens rather than damages relationships. Strong (effective) relationships bring a feeling of peace and freedom, a sense of accomplishment, and the excitement of doing "good" for others.

Declare Independence

Unbind the Shackles of Debt and Emotional Clutter

It is incumbent on every generation to pay its own debts as it goes. A principle which if acted on would save one-half the wars of the world.

Thomas Jefferson

A man in debt is so far a slave.

Ralph Waldo Emerson

Rather go to bed without dinner than to rise in debt.

Benjamin Franklin

Anything that we can do to raise personal savings is very much in the interest of this country.

Alan Greenspan

The time to save is now. When a dog gets a bone, he doesn't go out and make a down payment on a bigger bone. He buries the one he's got.

Will Rogers

Just as the rich rule the poor, so the borrower is servant to the lender.

Proverbs 22:7 (NLT)

Eliminate Financial Debt

The shackles of financial debt may merely impede progress toward your vision, or they may bind so tightly that you cannot envision a brighter future. Debt starts small, perhaps with one credit card or loan, then two...and if left untended it grows like a cancer until all your thoughts are consumed by fear, doubt, and insecurity. Debt today is far too commonplace, and, contrary to the proclamations of marketers and bankers, will stifle rather than help to achieve your dreams. Credit card debt, mortgages, second mortgages, car loans, and student loans all become anchors that threaten to pin you under the waterline, preventing the attainment of your goals.

When I was young, I was fortunate enough to receive academic scholarships from USC for undergraduate studies and a full-ride scholarship from Hughes Aircraft Company for my graduate studies. Still, when I entered the workforce, I had a couple of student loans, an automobile loan, and a small amount of credit card debt. My immediate dream (or vision) was to purchase my first home in Silicon Valley within two years of my graduation. Yet though my debt was not great, my income-to-debt ratio was not sufficient to qualify for a large enough mortgage to purchase a single-family home. My choices were to settle for a condo or town home, or substantially reduce my debt in order to purchase a stand-alone home. I could already feel the shackles of debt limiting my freedom and could not bear to further increase that burden. I chose instead to embark on a simple but disciplined journey to eliminate my debt. By following a simple plan, I was able to eliminate student loan and credit card debt within just over one year, and soon after, my new vehicle debt. This left nearly a year to add to my coffers for a down payment on a home.

If debt's manacles are impeding progress toward your goals and obscuring your vision of the future, it is past time to declare your independence by setting in motion an emancipation plan. Begin to eliminate debt and free your mind to develop a vision of your future. Without such a plan, you may find yourself in a crazy whirlwind, spiraling toward a debt-burdened existence or even bankruptcy, which may in turn hamstring any motivation to create a vision, improve your relationships, or contribute to the welfare of others.

I followed a fairly simple debt-elimination strategy that worked for me and has since worked for friends who were curious as to how I accomplished my goals. I determined my net income by subtracting withholdings (taxes, insurance, and 401[k]) from my gross income. My employer offered a 401(k) match, so I included a 401(k) withholding that allowed me to participate at a level that maximized the company match. "Take free money. No matter how in debt you are, if your employer offers a matching contribution on a 401(k) or other retirement vehicle, you must sign up and contribute enough to get the maximum company match each year. Think of it as a bonus." (Suze Orman)

Next I created a simple budget by determining my approximate fixed and variable costs. For fixed costs, I included all expenses that I did not have much control over: rent, utilities (note: one can strive to minimize utilities by employing sound conservation efforts), the minimum payments on debt, and so on. Variable expenses were basically everything else: food, recreational activities, vacations, gasoline, auto maintenance, household supplies, and so on. In other words, variable expenses scale with activity.

Once I had all this information, I determined if my net income minus fixed and variable expenses was greater or less than zero. You need to do the same. If less than zero, this value is called a "burn rate," and you need to reduce your variable costs. Next you need to divide your total savings by your monthly burn rate to determine your runway (the amount of time remaining until you "burn through" your savings). This is a powerfully simple method, though it is surprising how few individuals and companies track their runway when they get upside-down.

Once your burn rate is understood, take immediate steps to reduce spending on nice-to-have items rather than must-haves. Be honest with yourself. Going out to eat is a nice-to-have, not a must-have. That new video game or large-screen TV is not a must-have—no, you *can* live without them. Likewise, cable TV and Netflix are nice-to-haves. On the other hand, sufficient food, clothes, and shoes for your children are must-haves—whereas extra clothes, extra food, and extra shoes are nice-to-have. Be wise. For instance, it may be tempting to ignore the check-engine light on your car in order to take a nice vacation, but it is neither wise nor prudent. When you are upside-down, it is time to consider a staycation, reduced R and R, and reduced nice-to-haves. It is time to be pragmatically honest about must-haves. If you must have your car, then proper maintenance will prevent higher expenditures as compared with simply driving until a major problem occurs. Reduce nice-to-haves quickly and decisively, taking no more than one to two months so that you do not consume your entire savings.

When you are no longer upside-down, it is time to begin your debt-elimination process. For ease, assume your net income now exceeds expenditures by $200 per month. If you do not have any money set aside for a "rainy day," you should create an emergency fund. Some recommend approximately six months of expenditures in savings, but it may be a better idea to first target $1,000 minimum prior to reducing your debt.

Now rank your debts from low to high. Target the lowest debt to pay off first. Don't worry about interest rates unless you have two debts that are approximately equal; then first target to pay the debt with the highest interest. For example, say you have $25,000 debt at 5 percent, $12,000 at 8 percent, $1,000 at 12 percent, and $950 at 5 percent; then you would pay off the $1,000 at 12 percent first, followed by the $950, then the $12,000, and lastly the $25,000.

Focus on your goal, and make only the minimum payment on all other debts. All extra money will be used to pay down the $1,000 debt. So if you've been paying a $50 minimum per month on that debt, but you have an extra $200 monthly, you should now pay $250 per month. In four payments, you will have nearly eliminated this debt (for ease, we will assume the debt is gone).

Next, if the minimum payment on the $950 debt has been $35, then take the $250 now left over plus the $35, and apply a monthly payment of $285. In approximately four months, this debt will be relieved, with extra in the fourth month to apply toward the next debt.

Now set your sight on the $12,000 debt. If your minimum payment has been $215 per month, then you will have $285 + $215 = $500 per month to apply toward this next debt. But let's also assume that in the year since you started this process, you've been able to increase your positive cash flow by another $250 per month. It may be tempting to use this for fun, but hold true to the objective. Apply the $250 to your payment for a total of $750 per month, so you will eliminate the $12,000 debt in approximately eighteen months.

And now, assuming you have been paying $325 per month on the largest debt of $25,000, and that over the past eighteen months, you've achieved another $75 per month above expenditures, you will have $750 + $325 + $75 = $1,150 for your new monthly payment to apply to the $25,000 debt, which will subsequently be retired in approximately two years. By diligently following this plan, you will have eliminated your debt in just over four years. Of course, this is just one of an infinite number of scenarios, but this simple process is powerful and effective. It worked for me, and it will work for you.

This can be summarized as follows:

1. Determine your gross and net incomes.
   a. Net equals gross minus withholdings.
   b. Withholdings include federal, state, and local taxes; medical and dental insurance; and so on.
   c. If your employer offers a matching contribution for a 401(k) (or other retirement vehicle), participate to a level that allows you to receive the maximum company match each year.

2. Create a simple budget.
    a. Sum all sources of income.
    b. Sum spending.
        i. Fixed costs
        ii. Variable costs
3. Determine if net income minus spending (fixed + variable) is greater than zero.
    a. If not, this is your burn rate.
        i. Total savings divided by the monthly burn rate yields your runway in months. For example, if you have $1,000 saved and your burn rate is $200 a month, you have a five-month runway (five months until your savings are depleted).
        ii. Reduce variable costs by about $400 per month to achieve a positive cash flow of $200 to be applied to debt management.
    b. If fixed costs alone exceed your net income, you may need to seek professional help to develop a recovery plan. The bottom line is that a plan to live within your means (in other words, a plan to spend less than you make) is a must-have.
4. List all your debts and minimum monthly payments.
    a. Rank the debt from low to high.
    b. Pay off the lowest debt first. Determine how much you can pay against that debt (you need to stretch above the minimum due by reducing your variable spending). Pay only the minimum payment on all your other debts. Any additional income should be applied toward the debt you can pay off first.
    c. Once you pay off that debt, take the value of the last payment and apply it (in addition to the minimum due) to the monthly payment for your next lowest debt.
    d. Continue to follow this payment ballooning process until you have eliminated all debt.

5. Once out of debt, don't go back. Save.

Now that you are out of debt (except for a mortgage, possibly), start to work on savings. Hopefully you have been taking advantage of a 401(k) plan at work to receive the company match. Regardless, it is time to save—not spend. Take the $1,150 now left over each month and open a savings account. Target a savings equivalent of six to twelve months of monthly expenses. To achieve better returns, consider IRAs, mutual funds, or other investment opportunities. Check out DaveRamsey.com to learn more about investing and debt elimination.

Once you have tasted freedom from your debt, you will not want to go back. But desire without discipline is not enough. Maintain a budget to ensure you do not slip back into the mode of spending more money than you bring home. Use credit cards like cash by paying off the entire balance each month. It is possible to break the burden of debt and live more freely. If you have not already done so, it is time for your personal emancipation proclamation! Eliminate debt–be set free.

Eliminate Emotional Debt

Eliminating financial debt is the first step in freeing your mind to focus on your vision of the future. But eliminating emotional clutter is also necessary. The good news is that this process works in parallel with the financial debt-elimination process.

So what is emotional debt? Let's assume your subconscious mind can process a fixed number of items without losing track of important details. This limit is likely different for everyone, but once the number of items you are attempting to track exceeds your mind's emotional limit, you are officially in a state of emotional deficit. It is safe to assume that given our multitasking society, most of us are operating at some level of emotional debt. The instant you think about an idea, task or goal that requires your attention, the item is logged in your subconscious mind. If you think of a second item that requires your attention, your subconscious mind is now in conflict; both items are fighting for attention. "Remember me!" says one. "No, remember *me*!" says the other.

Interestingly, your subconscious mind is not good at prioritizing these items. Picking up eggs on the way home is tucked in the same file folder as finding a new solution to convert thermal into electric energy, or to develop a new gluten free cupcake. As more and more pending tasks are added to your mental in-box, your mind becomes cluttered and irritated. A process for eliminating the emotional debt is required to free your subconscious mind to work on your most important endeavors. How do you accomplish this? There is a simple (but not easy) solution: you need a trusted system to quickly and effectively store all your "reminders" so that your mind can be freed to create solutions and solve problems. Such a system will also assist greatly in the process of alleviating financial debt as you enter, track and execute your associated debt elimination tasks.

Recall also that relationships are key to our personal effectiveness. Financial problems and missed commitments or expectations are two primary causes of stress and conflicts in relationships. As a consequence, a system that is successfully in reducing emotional debt is one that will facilitate collaboration between family member, friends and colleagues, making it easy to set goals, align expectations and deliver on commitments.

Some say that a wholly paper system is most effective, due to the perceived complexity and cost of electronic systems; however, with the advent of cloud computing and the compatibility of applications across multiple platforms (personal computers, mobile phones, and electronic notepads), the equation has turned. Regardless, compiling all your pending tasks into one system will increase your effectiveness as long as you are committed to using that system. The ideal system is even a bit fun to use.

Before endeavoring to describe such a system, it is worth noting the common reasons that such systems fail to work for many. The most common cause of failure is living life firmly and squarely in the urgent.

Planning and organizing (blue-hat thinking—refer to *VerAegis Relationships*, Framework of thought, Part II) are important but not urgent activities. Unfortunately, when accustomed (also known as addicted) to constantly dealing with urgent important tasks, the last thing we desire is to allocate valuable *downtime* to important but not urgent tasks. In fact, as we become burnt out from the constant barrage of the important and urgent (firefighting), it is natural to seek refuge in activities that are not important and not urgent, which is the height of ineffectiveness. As a result, the proposed organization system needs to ensure that by allocating time to important planning activities (e.g., fire prevention), the time you spend working on urgent items (e.g., firefighting) will be reduced. A second reason many of these systems fail is that many people struggle to extract themselves from daily minutiae, so frazzled by constant bombardment and interruptions that they are loath to embark on "higher" levels of thinking for fear that they will crumble under the weight.

Thus, no system will work without an easy-to-follow process in place. The system must free your mind so that you consciously respond in appropriate ways to your task list. It must be a system that allows you to differentiate between the simple errand ("pick up eggs") and the complex project or goal ("develop a new thermal-to-electric conversion device"). There are many processes that work, so you will need to find one that works for you. I have used a hybrid system that combines various techniques I've developed and learned over time from on-the-job mentors, Franklin Covey training, efficiency zealots, and most recently, *Getting Things Done*, by David Allen. I will describe the process I have found easiest to implement and briefly share a system that I find to be quite effective.

I have found that most emotional stress (once finances are under control) is due to missed expectations, caused either by misunderstandings of established agreements, unrealistic expectations, an inability to deliver the expected performance on time, or a combination of the three. In many situations, these missed expectations share a common root cause: lack of systematic planning and execution, leading to mismanaged commitments. To reduce the emotional stress, one needs to do the following:

- Document a plan in a trusted system. Refine the plan until the issue is no longer consuming subconscious thoughts. For example, if the issue is keeping you awake at night, you haven't captured your thoughts appropriately in a trusted system.
- To ensure alignment of expectations and minimize possibility of future conflict one must clarify the commitment to the satisfaction of key stakeholders.
- Document your next action.
- Maintain commitments in a system that you review regularly. The system should do the following:
  - Alert you to upcoming due dates
  - Enable easy transfer of tasks to your calendar
  - Preferably allow you to toggle between higher-level goals, projects, and everyday tasks.
  - Enable you to create teams and collaborate with colleagues, friends, and family members to achieve your dreams and most important goals.
  - Enable key stakeholders and team members to view and comment on commitments.
- Facilitate organization and ease of information retrieval.

Ideally, goals are ranked via "weight" and tasks by due date and percentage of time required. Weighting (prioritizing) your goals may seem difficult, but it is highly illuminating and far from rocket science. I've found it to be most effective if the sum of the weights is equal to one hundred; so if one has five goals that are of equal priority, they should each receive a weight of twenty. If, however, one goal stands out as the most important, perhaps that goal should get a weight of fifty. Of the remaining four goals, there is one that stands out as being of the next greatest benefit, so it may be ranked with a twenty, with the remaining three each receiving a weight of ten. The advantage of this process is that it clarifies where you should spend your time and effort. If two of your goals are worth 70 percent of your "score," you need to make certain that those two do not slip. Furthermore, weighting facilitates alignment discussions with your boss, teammates, and key stakeholders to ensure expectations are in sync.

The optimal system will allow you to file your goals and tasks by team, department, and committee and to cross-reference them using "tags" such as *at computer, errand, call, reference, at home, at office, top ten, bucket list, worry list, family, friends, health, finance and accounting*, and so on. Such a system would automatically scour and rank by priority all of your goals, tasks, and projects as well as list your next actions and allow you to mark tasks as not started, on target, at risk, missed, partial, complete, on hold, or awaiting input. Further, with goals organized by priority, and with the next action listed for each goal, it is easy to determine if you are actually working on the items you have indicated are most important to your long term success.

Now what is the ideal process? It's one that you will follow, that works, and that is easily understood. Only you truly know the effort you are willing to commit each day in order to be effective. If you are motivated to get things done, have strong and healthy relationships, have peace of mind, and enjoy life, your process and system must be perceived as an overall benefit to you—helping you to achieve that which motivates you the most.

Start identifying and logging all the tasks that clutter your mind, your desk, and your counter tops. You might not collect everything in one sitting. Walk around your office and home or even your garage and yard, observing everything that might inspire ideas or tasks buried deep in your subconscious—bothersome when they resurface without warning. Let your ideas flow. Document them. If your mind is not at ease, document your worries. If you are still uneasy, read David Allen's

Getting Things Done for lists that are certain to provoke many thoughts.

1. Collect and document in one system (if possible) all the items that are fighting for your attention. It may be more practical to strive for one system in addition to your e-mail, but I recommend using e-mail only as your in-box and as a filing system for reference. Simply create topical folders (or tags, if you use Gmail) to store e-mail that you may desire to keep for future reference.

2. Position and detail each item. What does each entail, and what do you need to do?
   a. What is your next step?
   b. Are multiple steps required?
   c. When is it due?

3. Who, if anyone, can help?
   a. List key contributors and what they are responsible to accomplish (deliver).
   b. Determine if it is better to delegate the task or item.

4. Make it a habit to collect items, position them, and empty your in-box daily.

"Empty your in-box daily"—does it sound impossible? I had a colleague, Raj, who seemed to never have any e-mail in his in-box (though I knew he received fifty to one hundred new email messages each day. Until I learned his tricks, I was quite envious. He had a "touch once" policy. He read (or scanned) each message he received. If he was able to resolve the issue within a few minutes (two to three, usually, though David Allen recommends fewer than two), he did so immediately, then deleted or filed the original in a topical folder. If the e-mail required more time, he scheduled time on his calendar to address the issue, which is quite easy nowadays: you can just drag the e-mail to your calendar in many applications. This is useful for miniprojects, like editing an attached PowerPoint, Excel workbook, or Word document that may be important and have a specific due date, but does not require your immediate attention. In some instances, Raj would delegate the items in the e-mail to a subordinate or colleague. In summary, he scanned each e-mail in his in-box, and then either (1) deleted, (2) filed for future reference, (3) scheduled, or (4) delegated.

This same process that Raj employed for e-mail messages works for all the tasks and items that you collect in your in-box or task system (Figure 3). Why is it important to assess whether an item should be addressed immediately or scheduled? There may be many answers to this question, and an obvious one is that if you take the time to address all the items that accumulate in your in-box, you may never have time to address items that really matter. So a key factor in your decision-

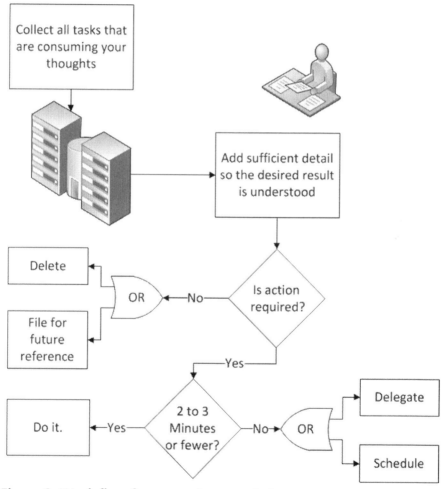

Figure 3: Work flow for managing your in-box

making process should be whether or not the task or issue is important. Answer this question while you are detailing the task: if the task or item is not important to you, why do it at all? The only logical reason I have found is that it may be important to someone who is important to you; therefore, you should complete the task for relationship management. Otherwise, delete it or store it for future reference. If it is important and action is required, do it immediately if is quick. Otherwise, schedule it based on both relative importance and urgency (note that not all important items are due now and not all urgent items are important!).

Imagine that the next task on your list, editing a large document, requires three hours of your time. The requestor does not require your feedback until late next week. You have several important projects for which you have scheduled time to complete this week, and today your calendar is swamped. If you work on the new project, you will miss commitments. If you leave it in your in-box, it will haunt your thoughts and potentially fall through the cracks. However, if you take a few moments to schedule the three hours required to accomplish the task early next week, your mind will be at ease knowing the time is allotted prior to the due date. You won't need to think about this again, because it is scheduled in your system; you will not be late.

You will be stressed when your actions are not aligned with your values and beliefs. You will be stressed if the weight of financial debt stifles creativity and imagination. You will be stressed if you struggle to remember all you have to accomplish—your contribution will wane, expectations will be missed and both your relationships and spirit will suffer. A fundamental key to a clear mind is to routinely empty your physical and mental in-boxes—implementing an organized system that can be shared with family, friends and colleagues (learn about a fully capable system created by Cloud Effective at http://www.CloudEffective.com). Once your mind is confident that you are out of financial and emotional debt, you will be able think about the bigger picture!

See the Future You Desire

The only thing worse than being blind is having sight but no vision.

Helen Keller

As selfishness and complaint pervert the mind, so love with its joy clears and sharpens the vision.

Helen Keller

All successful people, men and women, are big dreamers. They imagine what their future could be, ideal in every respect, and then they work every day toward their distant vision, that goal or purpose.

Brian Tracy

...You do such wonderful things! You planned them long ago, and now you have accomplished them.

Isaiah 25:1 (NLT)

My child, listen and be wise: Keep your heart on the right course.

Proverbs 23:19 (NLT)

Real, lasting contribution, the kind they will pine over in your eulogy, the kind that leads to contentment and a feeling of true accomplishment, is derived from identifying your inner dreams, your core motivations and desires, and then aligning with a higher spirit and making them all come true—improving the lives of others. Clear your mind. Dream. Pray. Think—deeply—and pray some more! The next steps down the road toward your lasting contribution are capturing the vision of your future, determining the path required to get there, and then setting goals to reach your dreams!

The objective of both a vision and a mission statement is to create a clear and actionable written testament that, when read, conjures images of the writer's ideal future state.

> **Vision**: what you want to become and what your aspirations are
>
> **Mission**: what your purpose and primary objectives are as you endeavor to achieve your vision

Vision statements are designed to inspire, whereas mission statements explain your compelling reason to exist and outline the basics of achieving your vision. Vision and mission statements should evolve from your strengths and capture how to best apply those strengths, leveraging competitive advantages (where you can be the best), key economic drivers, and core passions.

Vision Statement

In creating a vision statement, whether for an individual, a team, or an entire company, endeavor to capture the essence of what services or goods you are passionate about providing, who is passionate about receiving what you have to offer, and who is passionate about assisting. Your vision should outline how you meet needs and for whom, and what you plan to achieve. Succinctly put, your contribution is the difference you make. What positive difference can you make in someone else's life?

What needs do you satisfy? Two common types of needs are physical and economic. People and companies are motivated by needs of security, control, and fair treatment. Thus, you should strive to meet physical and/or emotional needs by providing solutions to problems in a reliable, consistent manner and with respect and fairness, so that any monetary expenditure seems reasonable when quality is compared with perceived value (the sense of value for any goods or services is proportional to the perceived quality divided by the price: value α quality/price). Quality is determined by how many needs you meet and how well you perform. Consequently, the value of your relationship, goods, and/or service is then determined by the number of needs you fulfill and how well you meet those needs, divided by the monetary, physical, and emotional costs. Armed with this understanding, you are in a position to create your aspirational vision statement.

Coca-Cola is one of the best-known icons in the world, and they assert that their vision is the "framework" of their roadmap and "guides every aspect of [their] business." Their vision describes what they need to accomplish in order to continue growing:

People: Be a great place to work where people are inspired to be the best they can be.

Portfolio: Bring to the world a portfolio of quality beverage brands that anticipate and satisfy people's desires and needs.

Partners: Nurture a winning network of customers and suppliers, together we create mutual, enduring value.

Planet: Be a responsible citizen that makes a difference by helping build and support sustainable communities.

Profit: Maximize long-term return to shareowners while being mindful of our overall responsibilities.

Productivity: Be a highly effective, lean and fast-moving organization.

Mission Statement

Your contribution is the difference you make. How can you make a positive difference in someone else's life? Remember that mission statements explain your compelling reason to exist and outline the basics of achieving your vision. What is your winning idea? How do you set yourself or your organization apart from the herd? Determine your strengths, and start there. How will you know if you succeed? What are the measures of your success? Do you measure your success by winning the state championship, the Super Bowl, or a beauty contest? Do you measure your success by the number of young adults who graduate from your high school, the number of sodas consumed per capita or per annum, or how often your children give you hugs? Your mission should declare your purpose and serve as the standard by which you test your decisions. If you require more assistance getting started, check out Franklin Covey's Mission Statement Builder at FranklinCovey.com. As an example, here is Coca-Cola's mission:

> Our Roadmap starts with our mission, which is enduring. It declares our purpose as a company and serves as the standard against which we weigh our actions and decisions.
>
> - To refresh the world
>
> - To inspire moments of optimism and happiness
>
> - To create value and make a difference

How does Coca-Cola measure whether or not they are refreshing the world? By the volume of Coca-Cola beverages consumed weekly, monthly, and yearly. "Refreshing the world" sounds much more inspiring than "selling soda to the world," but it can be measured by the latter's metric. Likewise, it is difficult to measure how "inspirational" Coca-Cola is, but with marketing and survey groups, they can receive feedback that "measures" the perceptions inspired by their products. And "create value"? Coca-Cola has been a great investment through the years and is one of Warren Buffett's largest holdings; though with the latest trends leaning toward healthier drinks and energy drinks, Coke's recent growth has been sluggish. But they have not lost their compass. They hold to their official values and are confident they will pull through this slowdown.

> Our values serve as a compass for our actions and describe how we behave in the world.
>
> - **Leadership:** The courage to shape a better future
> - **Collaboration:** Leverage collective genius
> - **Integrity:** Be real
> - **Accountability:** If it is to be, it's up to me
> - **Passion:** Committed in heart and mind
> - **Diversity:** As inclusive as our brands
> - **Quality:** What we do, we do well

Though sluggish, Coca-Cola has not lost its way, and Warren Buffett has not lost faith: "We've never sold a share of Coca-Cola stock and I wouldn't think of selling a share. When you've got a great business like Coca-Cola, the danger would always be that you would rest on your laurels. I see none of that at Coca-Cola. Tomorrow is more exciting than today."

If not heartfelt, visions are worth only the paper they are written on. The combination of a clear vision, actionable mission, and guiding values serves as a beacon in the night for any company, individual, family, or group that is striving to weather any storm, no matter how great. It is not a matter of having the "correct" vision or being "enlightened." Mere pontification of sound principles, in the absence of belief and consistent action, is shallow and hollow. "The crucial variable is not the content of a company's ideology, but how deeply it believes its ideology and how consistently it lives, breathes, and expresses it in all that is does. [Visionaries]...do not ask, 'What should we value?' They ask, 'What do we actually value deep down to our toes?'" (Collins 1994).

Visionaries create an atmosphere of trust, devotion and direction that is vital to successfully navigation through both calm and stormy seas! Twelve-year-old Mary awoke, but she did not feel as well as the Elk Grove Village morning was nice. Midfifties, pretty clear skies. Not much wind. No, Mary Kellerman felt sick. She crawled from her bed and made her way wearily to her parents' bedroom. She complained of a sore throat and a runny nose. Her parents comforted her, gave her some pain reliever, and started to prepare for their day. At 7:00 a.m., their world was turned upside down: they found Mary unresponsive, lying on the bathroom floor. Mary's father remembered that morning as follows: "I heard her go into the bathroom. I heard the door close. Then I heard something drop. I went to the bathroom door. I called, 'Mary, are you OK?' There was no answer. I called again: 'Mary, are you OK?' There was still no answer. So I opened the bathroom door, and my little girl was on the floor unconscious. She was still in her pajamas" (Politics 2012).

Paramedic Dave Spung arrived at the scene, quickly assessed Mary's condition, and then immediately rushed her to the emergency room. Just before 10:00 a.m., Mary Kellerman was pronounced dead at Alexian Brother Medical Center in Elk Grove Village. Nick Pishos, an investigator with Cook County's medical examiner's office, interviewed Mary's father over the phone and requested the police to confirm the facts with both parents at their home.

That same day, approximately eleven miles away in Arlington Heights, twenty-seven-year-old postal worker Adam Janus, who also felt ill, had to call in sick. Adam had just picked his children up from preschool and finished lunch when he decided to take a couple of Tylenol capsules and lie down. A few moments later, he stumbled into the kitchen and collapsed. Paramedics were summoned to his home around noon. They arrived to find him on the floor, his breathing labored, blood pressure low, and pupils fixed and dilated. The paramedics rushed Janus to the Northwest Community emergency room, where they unsuccessfully attempted resuscitation. At 3:15 p.m., Adam Janus was declared dead by Dr. Thomas Kim: "Our first job is to resuscitate, and we couldn't...do that. His heart just would not resuscitate. I signed [Janus] out as probably cardiac death. I was talking to his family, explaining—trying to explain—what had happened. It's hard even if you know the diagnosis. I was trying to tell them we didn't know why. Adam's wife, Teresa, was there. His parents were there, and a whole slew of other people. And they didn't go back to their homes; they went back to [Janus's] house in Arlington Heights" (Politics 2012).

Adam's family mourned his death that evening. They were devastated and confused. A massive heart attack at only twenty-seven years old? How? While they anguished over Adam's death, his younger brother Stanley, twenty-five, and Stanley's wife, also named Theresa, came down with painful headaches likely induced by the stress of Adam's sudden and unexpected death. They noticed the bottle of Extra Strength Tylenol on the kitchen counter. They each took two capsules and moments later collapsed. The horrified family once again summoned the paramedics. It was around 5:00 p.m. When Lieutenant Charles Kramer of the Arlington Heights Fire Department arrived, he found cars and people everywhere, with his crew of eight split between Stanley and Theresa, fighting to save their lives. The symptoms were nearly identical: whatever happened to Stanley happened to Theresa only moments later. Lieutenant Kramer called nurse Helen Jensen, who was the only public-health person he knew. She dropped everything and rushed to the hospital. Meanwhile, Dr. Kim was just leaving for the day:

> As I was putting on my blue blazer to leave, around 5:30, a nurse told me that they were bringing the Janus family back. And I said, "Well, it's probably the parents," because they were feeble and they might have been very upset. And the nurse said, "No, it's his brother." I had been talking to this six-foot healthy guy. And I said, "Well, what happened? Did he faint?" And she said, "They are doing CPR—and they are working on his wife too." That's when I took my blazer off. (Politics 2012)

At 8:00 p.m., nurse Jensen and investigator Pishos went to the Janus home in search of the smoking gun. At 8:15 p.m., Stanley was pronounced dead. Nothing jumped out at Jensen or Pishos as an obvious contaminant. They found some over-the-counter medications and some prescription drugs. In the basement, they found that Adam had some metal-working equipment and searched for potentially hazardous processing chemicals, to no avail. Then Jensen noticed the bottle of Tylenol. There were six tablets missing, with two people dead and a third, Theresa, not expected to live. With the bottle in hand, Jensen and Pishos returned to the hospital.

> Back at the hospital, Jensen plopped the bottle of Tylenol down and said, "This is the cause." At first she was met with skepticism. Dr. Kim thought, well maybe, but how? "I was pacing in my office. I kept going in my systematic way: What is likely or not likely? All I came down to was cyanide. But I said, "No! Where? Where was the exposure?" The only way I could test was to check the blood for cyanide. I had never done that. I'd never heard of it. We didn't do that in the hospital. Someone...told me about a lab that does those special tests. So I sent the blood samples away."

> Pishos met with another officer at the hospital to preserve the chain of evidence. He recalled Mary's death from earlier in the day, in Elk Grove Village, and that the paramedics had also inventoried a bottle of Tylenol. "When I got [the Tylenol bottles], I looked and saw the control numbers were the same. I reported back to the medical examiner's office and I said, 'Look, everything here is different except this: Both have Tylenol bottles, and they both have the same control number: MC2880.' I opened them up and looked inside. I poured them out. Nothing looked out of the ordinary. Everything was capsules. However, as I was pouring them out of the bottles, I could tell there was a strong smell of almonds. And then I opened the second bottle and I said [to Deputy Medical

Examiner Donoghue], 'You know, the first one smells like the second one: almonds.'" Simultaneously, Donoghue and Pishos said, "Cyanide." (Politics 2012)

By 1:00 a.m. on September 30, Dr. Kim received reports that confirmed blood samples from the Janus family members were tainted with massive doses of cyanide. Later that morning, Michael Shaffer, Cook County's chief toxicologist, completed his tests confirming that the Tylenol capsules were laced with significantly more cyanide than is required to kill an average-sized adult. Sometime before 10:00 a.m., a Johnson & Johnson attorney arrived at the office of deputy medical examiner Donoghue. They escorted the attorney to the lab and walked him through the evidence:

1. All victims had just taken Tylenol capsules.

2. Tests showed that their blood was laced with cyanide.

3. Tests showed that the Tylenol taken from the scene was laced with cyanide.

Imagine now that it is 10:00 a.m. on September 30, 1982. You are the CEO of Johnson & Johnson. You've just been notified by a corporate attorney that two bottles of one of your newer and best-selling products, Extra Strength Tylenol, were found to have been laced with cyanide and directly related to the deaths of at least three people, with one more likely and who knows how many more at risk. All of the victims were in the greater Chicago area. The FBI has advised that you should not succumb to this terrorist who wants to show how easily a major corporation can be brought to its knees. Prior to this incident, Tylenol was the number-one over-the-counter drug in the United States. What do you do? How do you respond? Do you have a compass to guide you through this tragic event? Do you wing it, making it up as you go? Surely you have a group of advisors—lawyers, accountants, financial analysts, board members, and investors—probably all providing sound advice, especially from each of their specific paradigms: *Move quickly to establish that the bottles were not tampered with during the manufacturing process. Try to keep this as quiet as possible so that the stock prices don't get hammered. Don't admit to any wrongdoing. Suggest that Johnson & Johnson products are safe.* And on and on. How does one filter through all the advice and make a sound and prudent decision based on lasting values and principles? Well, to start with, one should be already be well versed in and firmly aligned with the organization's values and lasting principles.

Johnson & Johnson has a credo. It does now. It did in 1982. In fact, one can find its credo on the Johnson & Johnson website:

> We believe our first responsibility is to the doctors, nurses and patients, to mothers and fathers and all others who use our products and services. In meeting their needs everything we do must be of high quality. We must constantly strive to reduce our costs in order to maintain reasonable prices. Customers' orders must be serviced promptly and accurately. Our suppliers and distributors must have an opportunity to make a fair profit.
>
> We are responsible to our employees, the men and women who work with us throughout the world. Everyone must be considered as an individual. We must respect their dignity and recognize their merit. They must have a sense of security in their jobs. Compensation must be fair and adequate, and working condition clean, orderly and safe. We must be mindful of ways to help our employees fulfill their family responsibilities. Employees must feel free to make suggestions and complaints. There must be equal opportunity for employment, development and advancement for those qualified. We must provide competent management, and their actions must be just and ethical.
>
> We are responsible to the communities in which we live and work and to the world community as well. We must be good citizens—support good works and charities and bear our fair share of taxes. We must encourage civic improvements and

better health and education. We must maintain in good order the property we are privileged to use, protecting the environment and natural resources.

Our final responsibility is to our stockholders. Business must make a sound profit. We must experiment with new ideas. Research must be carried on, innovative programs developed and mistakes paid for. New equipment must be purchased, new facilities provided and new products launched. Reserves must be created to provide for adverse times. When we operate according to these principles, the stockholders should realize a fair return.

Before the murder spree was over, cyanide-laced Tylenol capsules had claimed four more lives: Theresa Janus, wife of Stanley Janus, twenty-seven-year-old Mary Reiner, mother of four; thirty-five-year-old Paula Prince, a United Airlines stewardess; and the seventh victim, thirty-five-year-old Mary McFarland of Elmhurst, Illinois. Jim Burke, Johnson & Johnson CEO at the time, had to act fast and decisively. Prior to this tragedy, Burke estimated that he spent nearly 40 percent of his time communicating Johnson & Johnson's credo. When faced with the crisis, where did he turn? To the credo. Their first responsibility was to the customers who used Johnson & Johnson products. Some had died. Others were surely at risk.

James Burke didn't need to delve further, but if he did, he would have found plenty of material to formulate an appropriate response: "Be just and ethical...responsible to the communities...be good citizens...provide for adverse times." And finally, "When we operate by these principles, the stockholders should realize a fair return."

From this we can surmise that Burke and his company had the financial means to weather this storm. They were committed to doing the "right" thing, despite the possibility of short-term financial burdens. What did they do? At an estimated cost of $100 million, they immediately removed all the Tylenol capsules from the entire US market, not just the Chicago area. They mounted a twenty-five-hundred-person communication effort to alert the public and deal with the problem. They began work immediately on the tamper-proof (and childproof) packaging that is commonplace today. Stock experts were certain that Johnson & Johnson stock prices would plummet, but the opposite happened. The response by Johnson & Johnson inspired consumer confidence. When the news broke on September 30, 1982, the JNJ stock price opened at $2.75 and closed at $2.70. By the end of 1982, JNJ stock closed at $3.13, up 16 percent in just three months. Johnson & Johnson responded according to their principles and not only survived but thrived, despite the Tylenol "death in a pill" tragedy (Figure 4).

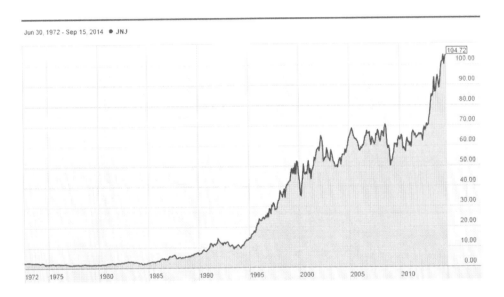

Figure 4: Johnson & Johnson stock price history (MSN 2014)

Take heart. A vision statement that is believed, acted on, and based on lasting principles can at times be motivating or at other times intriguing. But it is always a beacon illuminating your path forward, in good times and in bad. However, if the words are just words, then they cannot serve as a guiding light, and a ship once sailing strong and true can easily lose its way. Collins and Porras analyzed Bristol-Myers as a comparison company to Johnson & Johnson and included the following finding from a Harvard Business School case study: "[We] found no evidence whatsoever that Bristol-Myers had anything analogous to the credo until 1987, when it published the 'Bristol-Myers pledge' (which looks suspiciously like a paraphrased version of the JNJ credo). Nor did we find any evidence that the pledge, once stated, became anywhere near as pervasive a guiding document in Bristol-Myers. Whereas JNJ employees spoke explicitly about the link between the credo and key decisions, we found no similar comments by Bristol-Myers employees" (Collins 1994). In other words, it did not appear that the Bristol-Myers team internalized their pledge but instead treated it perhaps more like a sound bite or shallow New Year's resolution.

How did each company, Johnson & Johnson and Bristol-Myers, fare in the market over the past forty years? Figure 4 illustrates JNJ's performance in the market since the early 1970s: consistent growth from approximately $2.75 per share to approximately $50.00 per share through the late 1990s. During the first twelve years of the 2000s, riddled by the dot-com bubble bursting, the 9/11 tragedy, and the subprime mortgage crises, JNJ stock fluctuated between $50.00 and $60.00 per share, finally finding renewed growth in 2012, reaching greater than $105.00 per share in September 2014 and posting nearly a forty-time return on top of dividends since the Tylenol murders of 1982.

Figure 5 illustrates Bristol-Myer's performance in the market since the early 1970s: consistent growth from approximately $2.75 per share to a high of nearly $80.00 per share in late 1999. Both the dot-com bubble burst and the terrorist attacks of 9/11 rocked the United States, and BMY started a slide from their high of $80.00 per share to around $25.00 per share by 2002, and then to below $20.00 per share with the onset of the subprime mortgage crises—a four-time drop in price per share spanning a decade of crises. Recall Figure 4 and how JNJ weathered the same storm with fluctuations of approximately 15 percent. From mid-2009 until September of 2014, BMY stock recovered from approximately $20.00 per share to around $50.00 per share, at approximately 60 percent of the high mark nearly fifteen years earlier. Whether or not JNJ's vision helped them navigate the dot-com, 9/11, and subprime crises is not certain, but it is clear that both JNJ and BMY started at around $2.75 per share in 1982 and in 2014, were at approximately $105.00 and $50.00 per share, respectively. Johnson & Johnson provided over twice the return relative to Bristol Myers over the same period, largely because Johnson & Johnson weathered the storms better. Both companies enjoyed increased valuation when rising tides raised all boats, but Johnson & Johnson did not suffer the precipitous loss of value that plagued Bristol Myers.

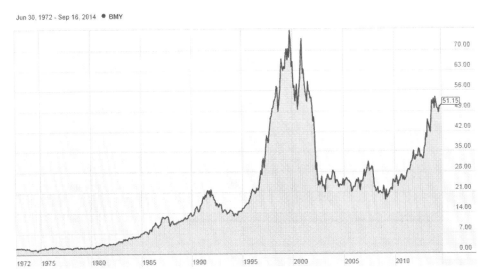

Jun 30, 1972 - Sep 16, 2014 ● BMY

Figure 5: Bristol-Myers stock price history (MSN 2014)

Have you written your personal vision and mission statements? Do you live them? Have you a vision for your family, group, team, or company? If not, are you ready to start? If you are not satisfied with your current situation, are you ready to rewrite and rededicate?

Think of some historical figures or friends and loved ones you admire—perhaps George Washington, William Wallace (Braveheart), Teddy Roosevelt, Joan of Arc, Thomas Jefferson, Helen Keller, Benjamin Franklin, Abraham Lincoln, Martin Luther King Jr., Winston Churchill, Martin Luther, Mahatma Gandhi, Mother Teresa, Jesus Christ, a father, a mother, an aunt, an uncle, or a childhood companion. What do you remember most about these people—the bookends of their lives, their opening and final scenes, dates of birth and death, or what happened in between? Life is what happens in between. One can either "go with the flow" or navigate to a desired destination, toward an ultimate vision. It is a choice. Real achievement, real contribution— the kind that touches souls and affects lives—leads to happiness and fulfillment, comes from identifying what you are called to achieve, your dreams and desires, and then working diligently to make them a reality. I challenge and encourage you to live beyond your comfort zone to be VerAegis! The first step is thinking hard about what you like to do or at what your organization is best. Ready to get started? On your mark, get set, go!

Play to Your Strengths

Most successful people are just like you and me. What sets them apart is that they've identified a talent and worked hard to make good use of it!

Walter J. Wadsworth

Knowing yourself and understanding why you think and behave as you do is necessary in order to enjoy positive self-esteem. Knowing others and understanding why they think and behave as they do is the cornerstone of successful relationships.

Dr. Taylor Hartman

Most individuals who lead rich, productive lives do so because they allow their instincts to guide them to the intersection of the head and heart, the place where their deepest passions and sharpest skills align with destiny.

T. D. Jakes

A spiritual gift is given to each of us so we can help each other. To one person the Spirit gives the ability to give wise advice; to another the same Spirit gives a message of special knowledge...great faith to another, and to someone else...the gift of healing. He gives one person the power to perform miracles, and another the ability to prophesy...someone else the ability to discern whether a message is from the Spirit of God or from another spirit...He alone decides which gift each person should have.

1 Corinthians 12:7-11 (NLT)

Successful people, teams, and organizations are those that have learned to exploit their strengths and heed their weaknesses. Your strengths, skills, and character traits are both innate and learned. Your deepest passions are products of your personality, which is part of who you are when you are born. Your character is likewise driven by your personality, your passions, and the external environment in which you live and work. According to Dr. Taylor Hartman, author of The People Code, each of us is driven by one of four primary motivations, and some perhaps by a primary and secondary motivation. These motivations are power (the motivation to get things done), intimacy (the motivation to cultivate deep relationships), peace (the motivation to live in harmony), and fun (the motivation to enjoy

If you do what you love, you'll never work a day in your life.

Marc Anthony

many adventures and relationships to the fullest). Our motivations fuel our deepest desires. When combined with unique (and honed) physical and mental gifts, our deepest desires make up the "instincts" that position each of us to succeed when we respond to our natural callings.

We are each born with certain motivations, as well as physical and mental gifts. Our behaviors, good and bad, result from our unique combination of circumstances, motivations and pursuant personality traits, both strengths and weaknesses (refer to *VerAgis Relationships*: What Motivates You?). Dr. Hartman's *The People Code* is designed to help identify core motivations and understand both positive and potentially negative personality traits. Physical and mental gifts become evident as one grows and learns. The key is to hone, improve, and exploit these gifts rather than neglect them or allow them to atrophy and fade. Recall the parable of the servants and their talents from *VerAegis—Relationships*. Talents were multiplied when servants invested and used their talents wisely; however, talents dwindled and were lost when they were buried and lay dormant. We each must learn to exploit our strengths, keeping weaknesses at bay so that they do not undermine our effectiveness.

Further, we are gifted specific strengths to complement the weaknesses of others. Teams are more effective when each team member utilizes strengths that augment rather than duplicate the strengths of other team members. Consider the human body: arms and hands are used for moving and carrying; legs and feet for walking, running, lifting, and supporting the body; the brain for thinking and controlling various movement and body functions; the eyes for seeing; the ears for hearing; and so on. Each of these body parts was given a purpose that, when fulfilled, serves the remaining parts. Aesop told a story of rebellion, "The Belly and the Members." In this fable, members of the body begin to feel that the belly (stomach, intestines, etc.) serves no real purpose and doesn't contribute to the whole. To the body's dismay, however, the members are terribly mistaken:

> The Members of the Body rebelled against the Belly, and said, "Why should we be perpetually engaged in administering to your wants, while you do nothing but take your rest, and enjoy yourself in luxury and self-indulgence?" The Members carried out their resolve and refused their assistance to the Belly. The whole Body quickly became debilitated, and the hands, feet, mouth, and eyes, when too late, repented of their folly. (Townsend)

The body members refused to play to their strengths, no longer fulfilling their responsibilities of finding and delivering nourishment: the legs would not carry the body to the market, the arms would not lift a fork to feed the mouth, the mouth would not chew, nor the throat swallow. Without nourishment, the body as a whole failed. It may seem simple, but each of us needs to identify our strengths and then use them for the betterment of ourselves and others—our family, teams and organizations.

For those motivated by power, you naturally push the limits and so are well positioned and likely love to conquer any and all challenges. You desire to lead, to be productive. You are undaunted by obstacles and derive satisfaction and joy from getting things done. Thus, you are often viewed by others as being incredibly productive and possibly as a natural-born leader. Exploit these strengths, but be mindful that you can also come across as a "bull in a china shop" with aggressive behavior. Your enthusiasm for achievement can make it difficult for you to be managed and to self-regulate. You may view authority figures as obstructionists, which is potentially volatile, because you are indeed undaunted by obstacles. You also have a tendency to resist assignments or tasks that you consider to be nonproductive, and unfortunately, when combined with your potential inability to self-regulate, that trait may lead you to fail to recognize the potential benefits of certain tasks. For instance, you might lump much of your relationship management into the nonproductive category. Your desire for respect and the need to be "right" and look good may also limit your ability to cultivate relationships, which are so key to achieving your personal best. Your bull-in-a-china-shop approach may lead to distrust from family, friends, and colleagues who often feel that you will shoot the messenger.

For those motivated by intimacy, you naturally connect with others and cultivate rich, meaningful relationships. You desire quality in both relationships and achievement. You are in all probability a good coach, and you seek to serve and improve the lives of others. You are likely self-determined and desire the freedom to do what you know needs to be done. You are wonderfully principled and doubtlessly have high moral standards, seeking fair treatment for all. Because of your principles, your focus on quality, and your nurturing nature, you are perceived by some as being a trusted, detail-oriented, and relationship-oriented leader. Exploit these strengths, but be mindful that you can come across as a "nitpicking perfectionist." Your enthusiasm for perfection, combined with your tendency to take the moral high ground, can at times make it impossible for you to get things done. Driven by a strong need to be understood, you have a propensity for waxing long and intensely, often coming across as self-righteous and aggressive. You may be prone to digging up the past and continuously searching for breaches of conduct that violate your principles and values, "knowing" that one more example is all that is required for others to recognize the error of their ways—all the while asserting that "recognition" of the problem is, after all, the first step to resolution. You also have a tendency to resist assignments or tasks that you consider to be for your sole benefit, and unfortunately, when combined with your potential perfectionist nature (you may think that if you cannot dedicate the time necessary to do the task well, why do it at all?), this trait may inhibit your ability to "sharpen the saw," leading to stagnation rather than continued improvement. Your desire for security and acceptance tend to hamper your ability to take risks or seek challenging endeavors.

For those motivated by peace, you are naturally "egoless" and particularly accepting of others. You desire independence, tolerance, and contentment. You are likely logical and highly self-regulated, with a natural gift for providing clarity even when faced with a storm. You are kind and likely positively interested in the well-being of yourself and others. Because of your accepting nature, you value diversity and seem to fit in with almost any team. Because of your astuteness and your ability to self-regulate, you are perceived by some as being a leader able to elicit the best from a team of diverse members. Exploit these strengths, but be mindful that your strong desire for peace can lead to conflict avoidance and passive-aggressive behavior. Likewise, your strong desire for independence, combined with your astuteness and logic, can at times make it possible for you to rationalize your way into believing that avoiding conflict is more important than achieving understanding and seeking reconciliation or resolution. Driven by a strong need for independence and autonomy, you have a propensity for suffering in silence and tend to avoid being "controlled" by the influence of others. You may want your own way in your own time to such an extent that you will make commitments without intending to follow through, just so that you can get on with your own agenda in peace and solitude. You may logically argue that these failures to meet commitments will be perceived as changes in priorities, but you run the risk of being perceived as someone with questionable integrity—possibly even someone who is duplicitous. Your desire to be left alone may hamper your ability to work with teams, lead, and resolve conflict.

For those motivated by fun and excitement, you are naturally outgoing and seem to have the world by its tail. You want to look good to the masses and can light up a room with a simple comment and smile. You are likely incredibly articulate and able to inspire others with both your words and presence. You are at your best when enjoying someone or something "in the moment." You desire freedom, happiness, and playful rather than challenging adventure. You attract others, and because of your ability to articulate ideas, your easygoing nature, and your ability to create fun, you are perceived by many as being a charismatic leader. Exploit these strengths, but be mindful that your strong desire for fun and playful adventure can lead to commitment avoidance and "suppressive" behavior. Meanwhile, your strong desire for independence and happiness, combined with your ability to make friends, at times makes it possible for you to rationalize your way into believing that avoiding conflict is acceptable, because you can easily find a new relationship, job, or situation that is conflict-free, even though you know in your heart of hearts that a conflict-free relationship is not probable. Driven by a strong need for acceptance, you have a propensity for withholding or suppressing fears, insecurities, and anger. Your need to be popular may limit your ability to discipline, which, when combined with your longing for adventure and your tendency to become easily bored—or even flighty—may hamper your ability to stick to one thing, work with teams, lead, and resolve conflict.

The bottom line is to know your motivations. Understand both your strengths and weaknesses, and create a plan to achieve your desired results. Regardless of core motivations, successful people have many common characteristics that they leverage to meet or exceed expectations. Recall (from *VerAegis—Relationships*) our vision of a successful person: a real (effective and balanced) man or woman is someone who values relationships; accepts responsibility; rejects passivity; contributes; leads courageously with consideration, passion, and integrity; and believes in grace and mercy.

Value Relationships

High achievers synergize with others. They understand the need to bolster their shortcomings with the strength of others, and they know that only by exploiting differences can they achieve synergy. This concept is not new. Nearly two-thousand years ago, Paul wrote: "For just as we have many members in one body and all the members do not have the same function, so we, who are many, are one body in Christ, and individually members one of another. Since we have gifts that differ according to the grace given to us, *each of us is to exercise them accordingly*: if prophecy, according to the proportion of his faith; if service, in his serving; or he who teaches, in his teaching; or he who exhorts, in his exhortation; he who gives, with liberality; he who leads, with diligence; he who shows mercy, with cheerfulness." (Romans 12:4–8 [NASB])

We each have different gifts. Groups, teams, departments, companies, and countries are better when differences are celebrated and each person excels in his or her area of expertise. Football teams don't ask their quarterback to block linebackers; guards, tackles, tight ends and fullbacks fulfill that purpose. Hospitals don't request that administrators perform surgery; they hire highly trained and specialized surgeons. Teams are stronger when they find differences and align each member's talent to his or her specific role. Value differences in your family, with your friends, on sports teams, and while working.

A good life is meant to be interesting, challenging, and fun. Life, unlike school, gives the tests first and then provides the lessons—so we must constantly strive to learn. Learn what others do well from their shortcomings and mistakes. Learn from your successes and mistakes. You were born with a unique set of gifts and instincts. As you learn from life's lessons, those instincts are honed into unique insights that, when combined with your God-given gifts, mold you into a truly special and valuable individual. To achieve success, learn to cherish your relationships, working with others to fully relish and exploit your unique instincts, insights, talents, and traits. Only then will you truly be positioned to provide a lasting contribution.

Accept Responsibility

People who accomplish a lot in life usually work hard. They do not necessarily have the most skills or talents, but talent combined with hard work and diligence prepares the successful to make the most of every opportunity. For the most successful, working hard does not just equate to working longer hours; it equates to working

> **Luck is a matter of preparation meeting opportunity.**
>
> Lucius Annaeus Seneca

smarter—setting goals and ensuring that time is set aside to work on the highest priorities. Being successfully means accepting our obligation to respond as necessary to fulfill commitments. As pragmatic optimists, we do not seek perfection but strive to do our best, meeting or exceeding goals and objectives.

Reject Passivity

People who are habitually successful find ways to consistently reject temptations to be lazy and rest upon their laurels. All people have God-given talents; successful people exploit theirs. To truly succeed, learn to reject all temptations to let your talent go to waste after enjoying initial success. When faced with barriers, high achievers do not become passive; they kick it up a

> **People who succeed in extraordinary ways are those who have found the few unique talents they possess and use them to maximum benefit. Talent, alas, isn't enough. Each of us knows people with talent who let it waste away. You must combine talent with a determination to use it.**
>
> Walter J. Wadsworth

notch, searching for a solution under, over, around, or through the most tenacious obstacles. High achievers don't just rely on their own understanding; they seek help from others. And believe it or not, family, friends, and colleagues view this as a strength, not a weakness.

My kids and wife enjoy humor, and have often said (just after something stops working), "Dad can fix it...Dad can fix anything." Once when Jimmy was about five and Teagan about eight years old, our television died. I opened it up and found that a transistor on the motherboard had fried. This I could not fix. I obtained a reasonable quote from a local TV repair shop. It seemed this was a fairly common problem for our make and model, so the shop had the part in stock. I loaded up the TV and returned a few hours later with the TV working as good as new. The kids were excited. Jumping up in the air, they shouted, "I told you—you *can* fix anything!" It didn't matter to them that I sought the help of an expert. In fact, they saw that as a positive, because the TV was fixed and I had extra time to play with them.

Don't go passive. Never stop using your gifts to the benefit of yourself and others. Never be afraid to ask for help.

Contribute

Those who contribute the most seem to have high expectations of themselves and others. They share successes, remain curious, and constantly search for new ways to exploit their talents. They are students of life, both learning and teaching constantly. They strive to be the best and to help others be their best. They do not obtain success by association but achieve real results by working with others synergistically to achieve more than is possible for individuals to realize on their own. They work smart and hard,

Life's most persistent and urgent question is, "What are you doing for others?"

Martin Luther King Jr.

yet keep gas in the tank for emergencies. They either instinctively realize or have learned that it is necessary to use their minds to the fullest—seeking to see the best in each opportunity, pragmatically analyzing risks, creatively pursuing options and alternatives, mindfully reviewing progress and data, organizing schedules, leading others by example, and finally doing a gut call: how do they feel about where they are in life? People who have found a way to connect with life have never strayed far from their gut instincts and core motivations.

Lead Courageously with Consideration, Passion, and Integrity

Recall the Stockdale paradox. Those who thrive are pragmatically optimistic; they face the brutal facts but don't become trapped by them. When bitten by a viper, they take the antidote but don't languish in sorrow and woes. Their motto is likely something like "plan, act, survive, and thrive" or perhaps "when the going gets tough, the tough get going!" They are determined in all circumstances that require determination, and rarely do they say, "I could have given more," or "If only I had..." They are passionate and act with contagious enthusiasm and energy. They thrive on challenge and change with such frequency that it appears they believe that if they stopped changing, they would drown or implode. They are committed and have honed the self-discipline to do the right thing, even when not being watched.

> **Discipline is the bridge between goals and accomplishment.**
> Jim Rohn

These people are generally honest, gracious, charitable, and noble. They believe that the quickest path to success is to avoid shortcuts. They don't move slowly, but they don't cut corners. They do not put off until tomorrow that which should be completed today. Aesop tells a story of "The Ants and the Grasshopper" that beautiful illustrates this concept:

> The Ants were spending a fine winter's day drying grain collected in the summertime. A Grasshopper, perishing with famine, passed by and earnestly begged for a little food. The Ants inquired of him, "Why did you not treasure up food during the summer?" He replied, "I had not leisure enough. I passed

the days in singing." They then said in derision: "If you were foolish enough to sing all the summer, you must dance supperless to bed in the winter." (Townsend)

Like Aesop's industrious ants, successful people understand that moving quickly in the correct direction is more important than speeding off down the wrong path, like the grasshopper who busied himself with nonproductive activities. Effective leaders understand the law of the harvest—the law of consequences. Effective leaders understand the adages "haste makes waste" and "don't be penny-wise but pound foolish," and when looking to heap praise for a job well done, they turn to the window, not the mirror.

Believe in Grace and Mercy

When things are going great, true winners praise the efforts of others, building others up to create an even more incredible team. Winners strive to make others look like winners. Alternatively, when mistakes arise, they question what they could have done differently to prevent the problem. They passionately search to understand the root cause, yet are composed enough to avoid placing blame. They humbly recognize that their knowledge is limited, and they are always willing to learn from others. As they desire grace and mercy in time of need, they generously extend grace and mercy to others in need.

If this vision of a successful person seems intimidating to you, don't be discouraged. This is indeed a vision, and probably no one fulfills all aspects of it all the time. But with diligence, we are able to move closer to the vision and increase the time between backslides. With sustained effort over the long run and extraordinary effort when the need arises, we are each capable of setting, prioritizing, and attaining our goals—and achieving our vision.

Set and Achieve Goals
Attitude, Plans, Execution, and Celebration

Learn from the past, set vivid, detailed goals for the future, and live in the only moment of time over which you have any control: now!

Denis Waitley

Setting goals is the first step in turning the invisible into the visible.

Tony Robbins

What you get by achieving your goals is not as important as what you become by achieving your goals.

Henry David Thoreau

The game has its ups and downs, but you can never lose focus of your individual goals and you can't let yourself be beat because of lack of effort.

Michael Jordan

In this life, we have to make many choices [decisions]. Some are very important choices. Some are not. Many of our choices are between good and evil. The choices we make, however, determine to a large extent our happiness or our unhappiness, because we have to live with the consequences of our choices.

James E. Faust

Whether personal or for your career, to set and attain goals is to manage change. Recall the see-plan-do-get change-management model (refer to *VerAegis Relationships*, Embrace Change). How do you see your world today versus what you desire it to become? How committed are you to turning the invisible into the visible? Who do you hope to become? Do you plan to achieve goals that will help you to become a better person and the world a better place or that will help you to acquire more material wealth? What is your attitude? Do you seek win-win or look out for number one? Will you take time to plan, or do you cut corners, jumping straight to execution because the solution is "obvious"? Do you strive to do it right the first time, measuring twice, then cutting once, or vice versa? Do you believe that planning is prudent and haste makes waste? Do you balance resources so that goals are achievable, or do you continually add projects and tasks until something breaks?

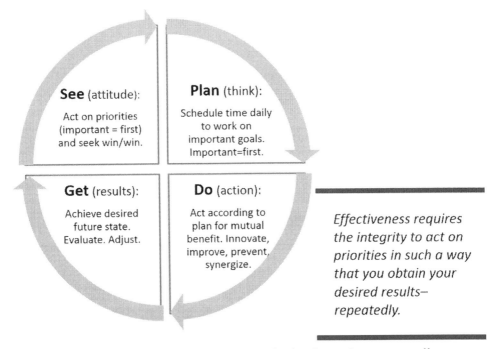

See (attitude):
Act on priorities (important = first) and seek win/win.

Plan (think):
Schedule time daily to work on important goals. Important=first.

Get (results):
Achieve desired future state. Evaluate. Adjust.

Do (action):
Act according to plan for mutual benefit. Innovate, improve, prevent, synergize.

Effectiveness requires the integrity to act on priorities in such a way that you obtain your desired results— repeatedly.

Figure 6: Effectiveness—achieving your desired results repeatedly— requires a pragmatic yet optimistic outlook combined with the integrity needed to plan and act.

The answers to these questions are indicative of whether you will achieve your desired results in such a way that you obtain them time and again (Figure 6). To successfully set and achieve goals requires a healthy attitude that embraces the idea that it is vital to act on priorities first and seek win-win outcomes. It requires planning, thinking ahead, and scheduling time on your calendar to work on important activities before the urgent has a chance to consume your time. In executing a plan, one must continue to seek mutual benefit, innovate, improve, and identify and steer around pitfalls, all the while seeking synergy with others. Finally, success requires monitoring results and adjusting as necessary.

Whether referred to as "WIGs" (wildly important goals), "BHAGs" (big, hairy, audacious goals), "SMART (Specific, Measureable, Agreed upon and Achievable, Relevant, Time-based) goals," "objectives," or simply "goals," the top priorities of effective individuals and organizations alike require a process for establishing, monitoring, and executing those priorities. Goals are a set of actions and deliverables that, when successfully executed, move individuals and teams closer to a desired future state. Goals represent our destination. However, the process of managing objectives and goals is not finite, with a beginning and an end; it is a continuous cycle that begins with high-level, visionary, long-term objectives (e.g., corporate or family objectives) that are in turn aligned with lower-level, shorter-term goals (e.g., department and individual goals). Whether for individuals or teams, goals are managed through project plans, shorter-term deliverables, and tasks. Project plans, Gantt charts, action boards, and the like are additional tools that facilitate the management and communication of progress. These plans are basically blueprints that detail scheduled actions and the resources required to meet the goal. Progress is routinely monitored (in terms of cost, schedule, and performance), and preventative or corrective actions are launched when risks are predicted or encountered. Once performance is appraised, the cycle continues (Figure 7).

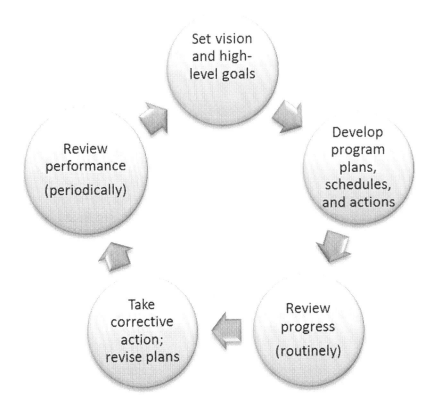

Figure 7: Management by objectives (MBOs) is a continuous cycle of setting and monitoring progress toward goals and an associated vision.

Donning our optimistic (yellow) thinking cap, we find there are several clear and real benefits to such a cycle: (1) high-level goals are aligned to department and individual goals, (2) resources are aligned to deliver for goals already established as important, reducing the need for firefighting, (3) team members understand what is required to succeed, since key shareholders agree in advance on plans and metrics of success, and (4) when plans are aligned, focus and thus performance improves at all levels, leading to a more satisfied and motivated workforce. Teamwork is improved. Results are delivered. We reach our desired destination.

Once deployed, the MBO cycle (Figure 7) changes the way time is managed: time becomes currency. The established vision and high-level goals set the direction that in turn directs your calendar. In other words, you and your teammates allocate time on calendars to work on top priorities, and the calendars dictate on which activities time is spent. This management process encourages relationship building by aligning objectives between supervisors, subordinates, and colleagues, providing structured opportunities to participate in decision making, alignment and empowerment, thus improving both ownership and buy-in.

Clearly there are many benefits to such a process, but there exist many potential stumbling blocks (time to don the black hat and employ critical thinking) that must be avoided up-front or corrected if encountered during progress reviews in order to reap those benefits. The first potential problems are those of attitude and discipline. Establishing goals and plans is a necessary activity; it is important, but it is not urgent, and it is an unfortunate reality that many prefer to put off until tomorrow that which could and should be completed today. We allow our days to be filled solely with urgent items, themselves often important tasks that were neglected to the point that they have now taken on urgency. These self-made emergencies (firefighting) are insidious, because they not only drive out important activity but also set the scene for future fires.

It is not effective to continuously prioritize the urgent over the important, and the subsequent stress leads to mental and physical fatigue (emotional debt). Stress drives people and organizations to spend spare time escaping both urgent and important activity. In other words, when taking a break from fighting fires, individuals and organizations don't rush to other important activities; rather we seek activities that are both not important and not urgent. We seek respite by squandering our precious spare time rather than spending it wisely on activities aimed at renewal, improvement and prevention of the next fire. Without improvement and prevention, however, future fires are guaranteed, and the cycle continues until one fire overlaps the next threatening physical and mental health of both individuals and organizations.

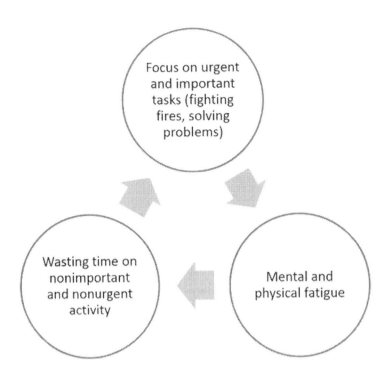

Figure 8: Continuously fighting fires and resolving mistakes leads to fatigue and wasted time.

To be effective, we have no choice but to break the cycle. Though weary from fire-fighting it is vital to redirect our spare-time to innovation, rejuvenation, and prevention activities. We need to focus on activities that are important, but perhaps not urgent (Figure 9). While it is valid and important to relax and unwind, we must avoid wasting time by sinking too much of our spare time into non-important activities that we may view as stress relievers. Remember, too much of anything is not good! When stressed from continuously fighting fires, we need to employ self-discipline and integrity to put important things first. Only then will we, as individuals and organizations, be able to break the firefighting cycle to consistently deliver desired results.

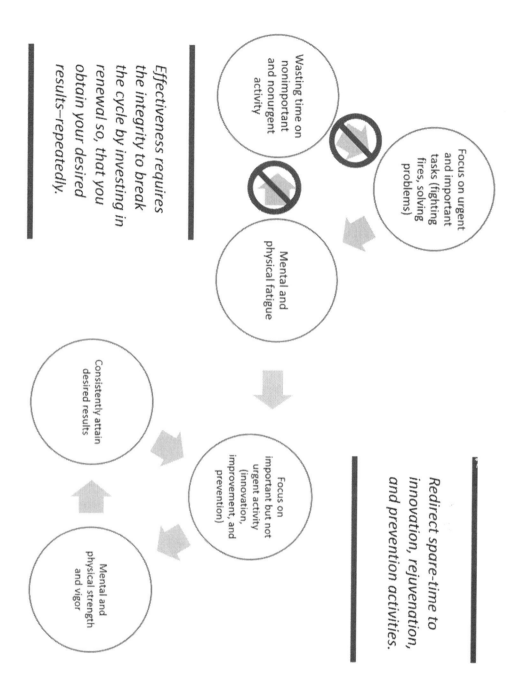

Figure 9: Trading firefighting for renewal yields the strength and vigor necessary to consistently deliver desired results.

There are additional potential stumbling blocks in the MBO process, but if individuals and organizations are on the renewal cycle, they will have "gas left in the tank" to understand and prevent or resolve any predicted or encountered problems.

Potential Management-Caused Stumbling Blocks

1. Failure to embrace the process and lead by example
   a. The MBO process is allowed to be perceived as "just another initiative"
   b. Failure to communicate hierarchy of priorities, failure to indicate both what is most important to do and that which will not be done
   c. Failure to gain "buy-in" and seek win-win
2. Failure to plan adequately
   a. Constant change of direction and priorities prevents MBOs from taking hold
   b. Failure to establish a hierarchy of priorities
   c. Tracking too much—for instance, tracking daily or weekly tasks as MBOs
3. Failure to execute and systemize
   a. Failure to empower the organization
   b. Too much "paper work" involved in performance management
   c. Failure to provide a workable system that includes management of both high-level goals and daily tasks
   d. Failure to drive accountability
   e. Inability or unwillingness to establish clear and concrete measures of success for each goal
4. Failure to monitor results
   a. Lack of follow-through once goals are set
   b. Performance-reward disconnect

Potential Contributor-Caused Stumbling Blocks

1. Failure to buy in and lead by example
   a. The MBO process is perceived as "just another initiative"
   b. Lack of ownership (buy-in)

2. Failure to plan and prioritize
    a. Failure to understand and embrace priorities
    b. Failure to translate goals into program plans and more detailed tasks
3. Failure to execute and systemize
    a. Lack of self-discipline in following the process
    b. Lack of constructive feedback to improve the process
    c. Allowing low-priority items (tactical minutiae) to drive out important goals by mismanaging one's time (spending time on the wrong things)
    d. Inability or unwillingness to establish clear and concrete measures of success for each goal
4. Failure to monitor results
    a. Lack of follow-through once goals are set
    b. Failure to proactively communicate results

See (Attitude): Embrace the MBO Process and Model Behaviors

The perception of the MBO process—the buy-in phase and resulting can-do attitude—is an essential element of the management-by-objectives cycle. Managers and individual contributors alike require pragmatically optimistic attitudes and the self-discipline necessary to own their slice of the pie. Emotional maturity is required for self-discipline. Recall that the criterion for emotional maturity is the appropriate balance of courage (and confidence) with consideration, kindness, and respect. The bottom line is to show others that you care.

Nobody cares how much you know, until they know how much you care. Teddy Roosevelt

If all members of an organization embrace a win-win attitude and act with high levels of courage and consideration, then all will be well; however, many stumbling blocks are encountered when team members clash. The clashes themselves are not the problem. Rather, the problem lies in the response to conflict. (Anger is not bad in itself;

it is the response to anger that matters. Learn more in *VerAegis—Spirit*.) In a sense, the MBO process needs to become a priority, and then, by extension, specific objectives within the process must each have a priority level. Mature organizations put important before urgent (and less important). Systems are deployed ensuring long term goals are fortified by shorter term deliverables and tasks so the organization is compelled to move toward its desired destination. Finally, a vital first step is establishing an attitude that MBO process is a win-win process.

An Effective MBO Process Must Be Win-Win

Take a moment to consider four possible outcomes of implementing an MBO process among management and individuals in an organization (Figure 10). In the first situation, perhaps the CEO crams the MBO process through, but neither management (Party A) nor individual contributors (Party B) seek to make the MBO process work. Management does the bare minimum to appease "the boss," and the individual contributors follow suit. As a result, collaboration, synergy, and sustained success are improbable, while the process itself is viewed dimly and considered another pie-in-the-sky idea, either dying on the vine or resulting in a wholesale change in the management team.

In a second potential scenario, imagine that one executive embraces the MBO process, but all others (Party A) are unsupportive. Though many of the individual contributors (Party B) seek to make the MBO process work, perhaps management does the bare minimum to appease the boss or ignores the process completely. As a result, small islands of excellence may appear, but widespread collaboration and synergy are improbable. Organization-wide, the process is viewed dimly and considered a marginal success at best.

Consider a third potential situation. Imagine that the CEO and executives (Party A) embrace the idea of an MBO process but do not put forth the effort to establish a process that can be easily executed at the working level. The executives desire a win for themselves to improve their access to data and their ability to drive execution, but they have failed to implement a process that yields comparable benefits throughout the organization. As a result, many of the individual contributors (Party B) rebel, while others approach the process with a lackluster attitude and cynicism. Management in turn expends excessive energy to keep the process alive, and while there may be isolated successes, widespread collaboration and synergy are improbable. Again, organization-wide, the process is viewed dimly and considered a marginal success at best.

Party A	Party B	Motivation	Results
Lose	Lose	Neither party is motivated.	Future collaboration is improbable; change is required.
Lose	Win	Only party B is motivated.	Relations are strained; future synergy is not likely.
Win	Lose	Only party A is motivated.	Relations are strained; future synergy is not likely.
Win	Win	Both parties are motivated.	Relations are healthy; future synergy is probable.

Figure 10: An effective MBO process seeks positive outcomes for management and individual contributors.

And now ponder a fourth potential scenario. Imagine that the CEO and executives (Party A) embrace the idea of an MBO process and engage individual contributors (Party B) throughout the organization to determine what is required to implement a successful process that can be easily executed at the working level. The executives desire a win for themselves to improve their access to data and their ability to drive execution, and a win for the organization in terms of providing mutual benefit—clearly defined targets and destinations. As a result, most (if not all) of management and their teams buy in to the process. They each have "skin" in the game and work together to keep the process alive. Initial successes are seen as reason to continue investment and improvement in the process, and soon, collaboration and synergy are flourishing. Organization-wide, the process is viewed positively, and future synergy is probable.

Win-Win Agreements

Win-win agreements are useful, and at times necessary, to turn a vision into a reality. Structuring a win-win agreement is not rocket science, and though straightforward, it is not easy. Win-win agreements require deliberate discussions to establish the desired results of all key stakeholders, guidelines of engagement, measures of accountability and consequences (both positive for successful execution and negative for failure to deliver). Stephen Covey covers the concept briefly in his book *The 7 Habits of Highly Effective People*. Win-win agreements usually consist of five sections: expectations or desired results, guidelines, resources, accountability, and consequences. Though not all situations require all five elements, I have found benefit in using each section in both personal and professional agreements. I've found it especially useful to set and agree on expectations, and at times, agreeing on the desired outcome (by creating agendas or action boards, and/or managing smaller tasks) was the only necessary step. Unmet expectations are the cause of many (possibly most) conflicts, and if expectations are misaligned, the chance of a mutually beneficial outcome is fleetingly remote.

In the fourth scenario (Figure 10), a business win-win agreement is helpful to define the requirements of the process and associated system, but before we jump into the details of such an agreement, let's review each element of a win-win agreement followed by a couple of personal win-win examples.

- **Desired results or desired outcomes**: Understand each person's hopes, and collect the desired outcomes. What does each party feel is necessary for a successful outcome? Note, it is reasonable to refer to these items as expectations, but at times it is better to downsize expectations to desired results or even preferences in order acknowledge the difficulty of the task at hand, and perhaps create a more trusting environment. The win-win wording creates the feeling that there is mutual desire rather than a top-down expectation—"He (or she) perpetually expects *this or that*...without realizing how difficult or unrealistic *this or that* may actually be!"

- **Guidelines:** Define the ground rules of engagement during execution of the agreement. Is there any specific team or organizational structure necessary, and are protocols or instructions required?
- **Resources:** Identify sources of support (human, financial, or other) that can be readily drawn from to achieve the desired outcomes.
- **Accountability:** Establish clear obligations for key participants. Detail the metrics of performance—how progress will be tracked and communicated, and how success will be measured. Establish evaluation intervals.
- **Consequences:** Capture both positive and negative ramifications of performance and outcomes based on established evaluation criteria.

Teagan's Win-Win Example

Teagan ran (waddled) into her preschool class as happy as a duck! She embraced the new experience: playing with friends, learning from her teacher and classmates, and being in a new environment with her cousin Sammy who was born a month earlier than her and with whom she had spent much of the first three years of her life. Sheri now had a few extra hours to spend with Jimmy, who was just over six months old and had recently began to crawl. Teagan's enthusiasm for school continued through preschool and kindergarten, but when it was time to begin first grade (full time and a new school), something in Teagan changed dramatically. Have you ever known or witnessed a child who could not leave his or her mother, latched on to the mother's leg and crying emotionally, "Mommy, Mommy—pleeeease don't leave me!"?

After three years without problem, Teagan became *that* child. We were confused.

About ten days before Christmas of Teagan's first-grade year, Sheri called to speak with me while I was at work. Exasperated, she explained that dropping Teagan off at school was too heart wrenching; Sheri was at her wit's end, and Teagan seemed to be an emotional wreck. Sheri practically pled, "What do you think we should do?" I attempted to calm her as well as I could over the phone and assured her that I would be ready to help after dinner that evening. I thought. I prayed. I heard the answer. I arrived home that evening with confidence. I shared my plan with Sheri: I was going to work through a win-win contract agreement with Teagan. It would be great! Sheri was surprised. "You actually believe you can work out a contract with a six-year-old?"

"Yeah...why not?" I asked. Sheri thought Teagan would get bored too easily and not want to sit through the contract "negotiations." This was good *critical* input. I put on my creative-thinking cap and developed a plan to make this a fun event.

During dinner, we told Teagan that Mommy would clean up after dinner because Daddy had something special to do with Teagan. Through the course of the meal, the anticipation and excitement grew. When Sheri began to clear the table, Teagan could barely contain her excitement. "Wait here, sweetie. I'll be right back," I told her. I dashed off to get my supplies: a piece of pink construction paper, a fountain pen (to raise her curiosity), some colored pencils, and a bunch of stickers. I was back in a flash.

Her eyes and smile brightened the entire room when she saw the art supplies. I briefly explained that we were going to work together to create a plan that would make the school drop-offs easier and enable her to enjoy school like she used to. She agreed to help and loved the fact that I would do the writing; she would do the decorating! We agreed that we would complete one of the five parts of the win-win agreement after dinner for five nights in a row.

70

To break the ice, I asked Sheri to share her desired outcomes for Teagan's education. Sheri, who was still clearing the table, smiled a perfect mom smile and gave the perfect-mom answer: "Well, I would like Teagan to make good friends and learn from both her teachers and friends. As she progresses through school, I would like her to become more and more independent, until she is able to live successfully on her own." I used the fountain pen to write Sheri's statement down as the first input under "Desired Results." Teagan added a few pictures and stickers of books, desks, and chalkboards.

Then I asked Teagan what she wanted out of school. "What do you mean, Daddy?" she asked. "Well, sweetie, what parts of school do you really like? What makes it fun for you?" That got the ball rolling. "I like my friends. I like recess the best! I like to play on the monkey bars and to play chase—that's really fun. I also like to eat lunch with my friends, especially when we eat outside!"

"Is there anything else?" I inquired.

"I guess I like learning too. Mrs. Weiss is a really, really good teacher, and she is really, really nice!" Teagan added more pictures and stickers of playgrounds, kids playing, swing sets, and monkey bars, and she ended by drawing a picture of her holding hands with her teacher.

By this time the kitchen was clean, and it was time for Teagan's bath. I thought we had done enough for the night, but Teagan asked if we could finish up while she took her bath. Sheri and I were pleasantly surprised by Teagan's enthusiasm and decided it would be best to take advantage of her energy. We gathered her toys, more colored construction paper, and some bath bubbles, and we were off. I sat next to the bath while she played. The guidelines to which we agreed were simple: maintain dry eyes at drop-off, kiss Mommy good-bye, then walk like a big girl into her classroom—no whimpering. The big aha moment came when we discussed resources.

"Daddy, what do you mean?" she asked as she played in the tub. I said simply, "Teagan, what do you need to help you get through the day without crying and wanting to be at home?"

"Oh, I get it, Daddy." She beamed. "I need a picture of Mommy and Jimmy. No offense, Daddy, but I'm used to not being with you 'cause you're at work all day, but I miss Mommy and Bo-Bo Boy (he affectionate name for Jimmy) during the day, and I don't want to be away from them." Sheri had just happened in to see how we were progressing; our eyes met, and she was off in a flash to find a picture. All three of us spoke more that night, and Teagan decided that if she could tape a picture of Jimmy and Mommy inside her desk, she would be able to look at them whenever she needed and not cry. Simple. Elegant. Would it work?

We agreed quickly that we would discuss the outcome of her day each night during dinner, and we would celebrate each success. For consequences, Teagan suggested and we agreed to several milestones for celebration (we assumed success and did not discuss any negative consequences). After seven consecutive days with dry eyes, we would go to dinner as a family at Sweet Tomatoes; fifteen consecutive days were to result in an ice cream party. One month without crying meant a small party and dinner at our house, and three months without crying meant a weekend camping with our family and both sets of grandparents.

Teagan made it through the next five days without crying. Drop-offs were a piece of cake. Then school let out for Christmas break. We hadn't considered Christmas break when we established the first milestone, but decided to stick to our agreement. Teagan needed two more days without crying in order to achieve her first major milestone and have dinner out. The first day back after Christmas break, Teagan broke down a bit at drop-off. Sheri reminded her of the picture in her desk, and Teagan gathered herself and marched into the classroom. That was the last day Teagan ever cried at drop-off or during school. Each day, her confidence grew, and at each celebration, she looked forward to the next. The agreement had worked. We had grown together as a family.

Jimmy's Win-Win Example

Jimmy has always been highly independent and a self-starter. He loves people and is motivated by fun and achievement—with an emphasis on fun. When he started high school, he harbored an unspoken desire to be more independent. Sheri had homeschooled Jimmy for his seventh-grade year, so was decidedly accustomed to being involved. Teagan, our daughter, is particularly collaborative and has always sought our input; given our familiarity with Jimmy as a middle-school student and Teagan as an extremely interactive older sibling, we had left unspoken our expectations of involvement with Jimmy during his important high school years. His and our unspoken expectations were misaligned and had led to a few confrontations between Jimmy and Sheri—and between Jimmy and me. This was not normal for us and not acceptable. We knew instinctively that the problem would get worse if we didn't act. Sheri and I met. We prayed and discussed possible approaches with close friends. Then we decided to work out an agreement with Jimmy. Sheri and I brainstormed ideas (refer to Unique Situations Requiring New Solutions) then, prior to meeting with Jimmy, we drafted a skeleton agreement in which we sincerely tried to imagine and capture our predictions of his desired results. We chose such an approach for two reasons: first, we wanted to show that we had listened and subsequently understood (or were close to understanding) his needs, and second, we were keenly aware that Jimmy would be much more receptive to a short, crisp meeting.

Sheri told Jimmy that we wanted to meet. I must admit, he was not extremely enthusiastic about meeting with us. It seemed he would have preferred a basketball game, a trip to Disneyland, or some other adventure—maybe even mowing the lawn—but nevertheless, he was surprisingly willing to sit down and work out an agreement. We were blessed in that he realized that in order to continue our great relationships, rather than navigating high school and his teenage years alone, it would be more effective to manage the changes he was experiencing as a team. We modified our agreement as we spoke. His input was thorough, thoughtful, and sincere. The agreement is still fresh as I write, but so far, we are progressing well!

Expectations and Desired Results

- Jimmy takes full ownership of all aspects of his academic and physical improvement.
- He learns the skills necessary to manage college studies and life beyond academics.
  - He studies each day (thirty to sixty minutes).
  - He completes homework (thirty to sixty minutes).
  - He does fifteen to forty-five minutes a day of physical activity (core and/or aerobics).
- When Jimmy does his best, works hard, and tries to enjoy learning, he will achieve his goals. (He offered and we documented his desired minimum GPA.)

Guidelines

- Complete homework, studying, and exercise before screen time (screen time is defined as playing with or watching any electronic device with a video display).
- Exercise when a break from homework and studying is needed—no YouTube or video games.

Resources

- Biology: Mom, Teagan, maybe Dad if you are desperate
- Math, physics, chemistry: Dad, Teagan, maybe Mom if you are desperate
- Papers and projects: Mom, Dad, and Teagan
- English and Spanish: Mom, Dad, and Teagan
- Bible: Teagan, Mom, and Dad
- Physical fitness: walks, weights, ropes, jogging, b-ball: Teagan, Dad, or Mom

- Jimmy will have Mom, Dad, or Teagan review papers, projects, and homework.
- Jimmy will discuss with Mom or Dad the attainment of objectives.
- He will use his planner, Cloud Effective, or both to plan ongoing studying, projects, and papers, changing the status as necessary for weekly reviews with Mom and/or Dad.
- Jimmy and Mom will review online grades together weekly.

Consequences

- We agreed on a monetary value per A.
- We agreed on a higher value (around twice as much) for straight As, plus dinner out for the family at a restaurant of Jimmy's choosing.
- Screen time:
  - No physical activity equals no screen time.
  - Minimum of sixty minutes studying plus homework before screen time on a school day.

Example of a Win-Win Agreement for an MBO Process

In the fourth scenario (Figure 10), a win-win agreement between management and the work force is used to define the requirements of the MBO process and associated system. The following is an example of such an agreement from a fictitious company called ABC Organization.

Desired Results

ABC Organization identifies and acts on the highest priorities in a manner that ensures continued success. High-level goals are aligned to department, and department, to individual goals. Resources are aligned to deliver against goals that are established in advance. Plans are created in advance of actions. Key shareholders and team members understand and agree to what is required to succeed. When plans are aligned, focus and, thus, performance improve at all levels, leading to a more satisfied and motivated workforce. Teamwork is improved, and synergy is achieved.

Guidelines

ABC Organization maintains and improves one MBO process. All executives, supervisors, and individual contributors will use the aforementioned process. Waiting for a perfect MBO process is not an option—we will begin with "good enough" and then employ continuous improvement. All constructive suggestions will be considered. The MBO system will be easy to use, intuitive, and affordable, ideally handling goals, projects, and tasks. High-level company goals will be cascaded down into the organization to ensure alignment of resources. Concurrently, individuals will compose goals and tasks, which will be reviewed and aligned with their respective supervisors. All gaps between tops down and bottoms up objectives will be discussed and resolved. Performance will be evaluated based on competence (delivery of results) and character (how you get the job done).

We will practice exception management at all levels; meaning accountability reviews, while noting and celebrating successes, will focus on goals, deliverables, and tasks that are at risk of missing performance, cost, or schedule expectations. Mitigation plans will be launched as necessary.

Resources

ABC Organization will use Cloud Effective Productivity Pro to administer our MBO process—to capture team missions, goals, projects, and tasks. Training material will be provided for SMART goals, project management, and performance appraisals.

Accountability

Each ABC employee is accountable for independently monitoring daily progress toward tasks and goals. Supervisors will meet weekly to review progress. Project team leaders will review progress and formulate plans and team action boards as needed—likely weekly, but possibly more or less frequently. Supervisors will conduct a midyear review with employees in July and a yearly review no later than February. Each employee is accountable for ensuring the ABC MBO process is a source of competitive advantage and does not become an overly bureaucratic burden.

Consequences

Execution of such an MBO process will help ABC achieve its vision of creating value, achieving profit, providing a satisfying work environment, and giving back to the community. Employees will become shareholders through our incentive stock-option program. We are a meritocracy. Performance appraisals and subsequent compensation adjustments will be linked to effective and successful completion of goals. ABC will set aside 5 percent of profit to share with employees and 5 percent to donate to select nonprofit organizations. Upon achieving an established percentage of our yearly goals, we will hold yearly celebrations at each site.

This win-win agreement established between executives and the organization is similar to the agreements between Sheri, me and our children—with clearly defined criteria, attainment of mutual benefit is not only possible, but quite probable.

Clearly, management and individuals alike must embrace a process by which to set and achieve goals. This holds true for both business and personal goals. Proper attitude is necessary but not sufficient alone to ensure success. However, if you think you are going to fail, you already have. Attainment of desired results requires a can-do attitude, organization, planning, prioritization and the self-discipline to turn "know-how" into "will do."

Plan and Prioritize

As we have discussed, effective goal management requires (1) the belief that goals are important, (2) the realization that not all goals are of equal importance, (3) a vision of the desired outcome, and (4) the necessary discipline to plan, schedule, and act on priorities (Figure 10). Setting priorities clarifies where the greatest amount of effort should be expended, which in turn facilitates decisions on how to spend one's time each and every day. As part of the prioritization process, individuals or an organization's leaders need to determine not only how chosen projects should be ranked

A man does what he must— in spite of personal consequences, in spite of obstacles and dangers and pressures—and that is the basis of all human morality.
Winston Churchill

relative to one another based on agreed upon metrics, but just as importantly, which projects will not be pursued. Too many organizations spread resources thin by simultaneously tackling too many opportunities, largely due to the fear of missing out (loss aversion).

Project Selection

A healthy goal-management process clarifies priorities and delineates which are the most important results that need to be delivered. An effective project-selection process is key to the successful management of goals and helps determine what to do and what not to do. Such a process needs to be easy to administer and update as time progresses. I have seen many project-selection processes that ranked projects based on net present value (NPV), return on investment (ROI), and perhaps a risk ratio based on the best-case three- and six-year NPVs divided by the worst-case three- and six-year NPVs, respectively. The financial analysis necessary to build models and calculate these ratios present a significant barrier to many projects and often require a designated team to perform significant "discovery" work that may not be merited by the opportunity. Further, these metrics alone do nothing to address the alignment of the project to core competencies, feasibility, and strategies. A simpler and more expeditious process is described below. It works well as a first step and helps to determine if a new process- or product-development team should be formed to dig deeper into the financial benefits and risks of each program.

The first step is to agree on benefit and feasibility metrics. These metrics will be employed to rank proposed projects relative to one another. Benefit metrics indicate how proper execution of each project will provide benefit to you or your organization. Examples of project benefit metrics are income or revenue growth, gross margin improvement, consumption of finished goods inventory, improved revenue per employee, improved profitability, utilization of existing capacity, and applicability to internal customers for vertical integration. Feasibility metrics, on the other hand, assess the ease of execution in terms of, for instance, how well the requirements are understood, buy-in from key stakeholders, availability of required resources, and budget. The concept can be demonstrated with existing resources and capabilities, the time required to generate revenue, low cost to entry, and so on. Of course, for home or school projects, these benefit and feasibility metrics will vary. For instance, in juggling home improvement projects, you may choose health, recreation, safety, and home resale value as benefits, and affordability, time to complete, disruption, and capability/availability (of your team or contractors) as measures of feasibility. Once you've generated your list of metrics, rate the relative importance of each. To drive differentiation, I prefer to use a one-three-nine scale representing low, medium, and high importance (Figure 11).

Next you need to choose the projects you will rank, taking care to select projects that will be handled by the same pool of resources (people, finances, facilities, etc.). In a development and manufacturing business, the projects might include qualifying an existing product for a new customer; developing a new product from existing processes and platforms; developing a new product from yet-to-be-developed processes and platforms; or reducing waste, material cost, and labor required in the production of existing products. Projects around the home might include remodeling a bathroom or kitchen, painting the

Benefit metrics	Relative weight	Feasibility metrics	Relative weight
Consumes finished goods inventory	9	Project requirements well understood	9
Revenue growth	9	Stakeholder buy-In	9
Gross margin improvement	9	Required resources are available	9
Improved profitability	9	Costs are budgeted	9
Improved revenue per employee	3	Feasibility easily demonstrated with standard tools	3
Applicable across many markets	3	Time to revenue	3
Fills underutilized capacity	3	Low cost entry	3
Applicable to internal customers	1	Requires no additional hires	3
		Requires no additional capital purchases	3

Figure 11: Weighted project benefit and feasibility evaluation metrics

exterior of your house, or landscaping your yard. Whatever the projects being considered, add them to a list and then evaluate each with respect to the benefit and feasibility metrics (Figure 12 and Figure 13). Again, to drive differentiation, I prefer to use a one-three-nine scale representing low, medium, and high correlation between the project and the corresponding benefit. Often, there is a need to include a score of zero, because a certain benefit or feasibility metric may have no impact on one or more of the projects. In our example, only the customer qualification for an existing product will consume finished goods inventory; therefore, all other projects received a score of zero relative to this metric (Figure 12). A score of one indicates minimal impact, whereas nine is extremely beneficial or has high impact (the project to qualify a new customer for an existing product promises to consume a lot of finished goods inventory).

Benefit metrics →	Consumes finished goods inventory	Revenue growth	Gross margin improvement	Improved profitability	Improved revenue per employee	Applicable across many markets	Fills underutilized capacity	Applicable to internal customers	Score
Relative weight →	9	9	9	9	3	3	3	1	
New customer qualification for existing product	9	3	3	3	3	0	3	0	180.0
New product based on existing platforms	0	3	9	9	3	3	3	3	219.0
New product, new platforms	0	3	9	9	3	1	1	1	205.0
Reduce BOM cost for existing product	0	3	3	3	3	3	3	3	111.0
Increase yield of existing product	0	3	3	3	3	3	3	3	111.0
Decrease labor required for top two products	0	3	3	3	1	1	1	1	91.0

(Projects — Total project benefit)

Rate each project with respect to each metric: 0 = no impact   1 = weak   3 = moderate   9 = strong impact

Figure 12: Relative benefit of each project, determined by the sum of the product weights multiplied by the impact score

The total benefit score for each project is obtained by multiplying each attribute's score by its weight and then summing the products.

Similarly, a score of one, three, or nine indicates low, medium, and high correlation between the project and the associated feasibility metric (one has low correlation, whereas nine has high correlation). In our example, the new customer qualification project received nines across the board, because the project requirements are well understood, there is great buy-in from the team members, and so on.

Feasibility metrics →	Project requirements well understood	Stakeholder buy-In	Required resources are available	Costs are budgeted	Feasibility easily demonstrated w/standard tools	Time to revenue	Low cost entry	Requires no additional hires	Requires no additional capital purchases	Score
Relative weight →	9	9	9	9	3	3	3	3	3	
New customer qualification for existing product	9	9	9	9	9	9	9	9	9	459.0
New product based on existing platforms	3	3	3	3	3	3	3	3	9	171.0
New product, new platforms	1	1	1	1	3	1	1	3	1	63.0
Reduce BOM cost for existing product	9	3	3	3	3	3	9	9	9	261.0
Increase yield of existing product	9	3	3	3	3	3	3	9	3	225.0
Decrease labor required for top two products	3	3	3	3	1	3	3	3	1	141.0

(Projects — Total project feasibility)

Rate the correlation of each project to each metric: 1 = low   3 = medium   9 = high

Figure 13: Relative feasibility of each project, determined by the sum of the products of weights multiplied by the feasibility scores

The total feasibility score for each project is obtained by multiplying each attribute's score by its weight and then summing the products.

By comparing the tables in figures 13 and 14, you might be able to sort the projects into various groups and define next steps; however, I prefer a graphical solution. At this point, I suggest creating an x-y plot of feasibility versus benefit. Such a graph, I have found, enables teams to organize projects into three distinctive groups (go, evaluate, and hold) pretty quickly and most often without argument. If any member disagrees with the outcome (if dissent occurs, it is usually among projects that fall into the hold category), the team simply reviews the metrics to determine if any adjustments are necessary. Are any key metrics missing? Is there general consensus regarding the weights and ratings (Figure 14)?

Figure 14: Project selection evaluation chart: ease of execution versus expected benefits

The outcome for our list of example projects resulted in one on hold, one a go, and four requiring more information. Qualification of an existing product for a new customer received an immediate green

82

light; though only third on the benefit scale, it is considered highly feasible and so represents the best "bang for the buck" without further analysis. The project to reduce manual labor required for the top two products fell into the hold category, scoring lowest on the benefit scale and second lowest on feasibility. Reviewing the metrics, we find that limited payback potential, high capital costs and the requirement with need to purchase new equipment in order to prove feasibility are the main causes of this project being placed on hold prior to time consuming financial modelling. Two of the four remaining projects are to develop new products, and based on the initial evaluation, are likely candidates for the discovery phase of a new product-development process which will require more rigorous planning and financial modelling. Meanwhile, the remaining two projects appear to be continuous improvement projects and are viable candidates for continued evaluation to better determine if the return on investment is likely to be favorable.

Project Management

The term *project management* may be intimidating, but everyone instinctively knows how to plan and manage projects. For the sake of this discussion, a *project* is defined as "a series of related tasks that are executed in order to achieve a specific desired result or outcome." Each day, you perform many simple projects without any "serious" planning, and it is worthwhile to analyze this instinctive process simply to reveal that the common capacity to plan and execute routine projects is strikingly similar to the process required to manage more intricate projects.

Consider for our project the series of tasks executed in order to start your day. Each person's routine varies, so modify the steps in your mind as you read. The first step may occur in the evening, when you think of the next day and set your alarm to awaken you at the correct time. Your alarm wakes you up. Do you need a snooze? If yes, how will you make up the time so that you stay on schedule? Your mind rapidly evaluates the options and ramifications. You decide and move on.

Upon rising from bed, your first stop is the kitchen, to start the coffee brewing. Grind the beans, grab the filter, add the water, and push start. Move on. While the coffee is brewing, you exercise for fifteen minutes and grab the morning paper. Then you have a cup of coffee while listening to the traffic report. Next you shower, get dressed, check the traffic report again, pour more coffee into a travel mug, and decide to pick up some bagels and fruit for your morning meeting when you stop for gas on the way to the office. You tote the bagels, fruit, coffee, and your computer into the office, quickly arrange the conference room, release a deep sigh of relief, and then enjoy an exhilarating jolt of confidence just as your colleagues begin to arrive. You have started your day and completed the project of simply getting to work on time and ready to go.

From this simple example we are able to define the elements of a project:

1. Define the project (objective or purpose, background, and desired outcomes)
2. Form a team
3. Brainstorm solutions
4. Plan and organize steps
5. Execute, monitor, and steer progress
6. Celebrate

Defining the Project

The first step is defining the purpose or objective of your project. What do you hope to accomplish? Employ optimistic (yellow-hat, Refer to *VerAegis—Relationships*, The Framework of Thought, Part II: Put on your thinking caps! Refer also to Figure 15.) and data-driven, analytical (white-hat) thinking to define potential outcomes. Recall that the yellow hat symbolizes sunshine; it is optimistic and focused on benefits, dealing with the positive side of why something should be done based on logical (not emotional) thinking. Use this thinking to document your purpose—why you're doing the project. Unless it's

84

mandatory, don't start a project if you aren't excited about it or if you don't have a favorable view of the potential outcomes.

Next use analytical thinking to list pertinent background information. Then use both optimistic and analytical thinking to define what you need to achieve in order to be successful (desired outcomes) and to determine how you will measure success (metrics). Most (if not all) metrics fall into one of three categories: cost, schedule, or performance. Cost metrics may fall into two categories: the first is the cost of your project, and if the desired outcome is to develop a product or service for sale, then the second cost metric is that of the service or product. Performance metrics are varied and at times easily quantifiable (size, power, speed, weight, efficiency, revenue, cost, etc.), while at other times, they consist of qualitative attributes that are not as easily measured (stakeholder buy-in; a fun, favorable atmosphere; team collaboration, etc.).

Yellow Hat— *Optimistic Thinking*: Focus on benefit, value, and why something may work.

Black Hat— *Critical Thinking*: Focus on problems, difficulties, and why something may fail.

Red Hat—*Emotional Thinking*: Focus on insight, hunches, gut instinct, intuition and feelings.

White Hat—*Analytical Thinking*: Focus on data, data analysis, information known or needed.

Green Hat—*Creative Thinking*: Focus on creativity, alternative solutions, and new ideas.

Blue Hat—*Organized Thinking*: Focus on organization of thought (order of hats to wear), process, actions, next steps.

Figure 15: Summary of six types of thought

The project definition for the "get to work on time" project might look like this:

Objective (purpose): Routinely arrive at work on time, invigorated and ready to go

Background: I have just transitioned from the role of individual contributor to project lead, and others are relying on me to be ready to lead first thing in the morning.

Desired outcome: Arrive to work on time (metric: frequency of on-time arrivals), ready to start the meeting before others arrive (metric: frequency of preparedness). Be relaxed, confident, and ready to lead. (These are red-hat feelings or qualitative attributes, which are not easily measured. However, a rising stress level is a potential warning signal that you are missing these desired outcomes.)

Consider a project you have in the near future or even a project you have completed in the past. How did it go? Have you ever purchased an automobile or a home? Have you planned a wedding for yourself or someone else? Have you completed a project for school or a science fair? Think about the purpose, background, and the desired outcomes for the project of your choice. Jot down these three elements of your project definition. Keep it simple and concise. Did (do) you have a budget and a schedule to maintain? Did (do) you have any performance measures to deliver? How did (will) you measure success?

Forming a Team

The next step is to form your team. In order to position yourself for success, you need the right people for the right amount of time. Thus, you need to define the skills necessary to achieve your desired outcomes and estimate how much time is required from each skill set over the duration of your project. Once you have a general understanding of the skill and time requirements, determine whom you know who is capable, willing, and available. In the "get to work on time" project, no outside resources were required, but that could change with circumstances. For instance, if you have a significant other or roommate, you might share responsibilities for making the coffee and breakfast; if you're part of a car pool, you might share driving responsibilities; or maybe you need an accountability partner to ensure you maintain your morning workouts.

Brainstorming Solutions

Review your project definition with the entire team and brainstorm how you can achieve the desired results together. Stick to creative and optimistic (green- and yellow-hat) thinking during the first phase of brainstorming, holding critical (black-hat) thinking for the second phase. Once it appears you have exhausted new ideas, organize (blue hat) the input into specific categories, such as approach one, approach two (usually the team chooses a descriptive name for each approach), additional resources, materials, processes, and so forth.

With a rough plan of how you will proceed, it is time to don the critical (black) thinking cap. Ask the team to determine what could go wrong that might prevent success. Document the results. Associate each potential problem to one of the existing categories, only creating a new category if absolutely necessary. The final step of your brainstorming process is to use creative thinking to identify actions designed to avoid potential pitfalls identified during the critical-thinking process. Considering the "get to work on time" project, for example, you might brainstorm several approaches to your commute: driving to work alone, carpooling, using rapid transit, or biking. Driving alone may be the most flexible option and provide some time to think, but it uses more natural resources and is worse for the environment. Utilizing rapid transit affords time to work using your laptop during your commute and uses shared resources but takes longer and requires you to walk the final several blocks, which risks dirtying your work clothes in the rain and snow. Riding your bike combines your workout and commute but makes it difficult to tote your computer and nice work attire back and forth from the office; it is also difficult to ride your bike in the rain and snow. Carpooling is a good option, but like riding your bike or taking public transit, it leaves you without a car to commute between sites throughout the day. Upon evaluation, perhaps the brainstorming leads to a hybrid option: drive to work each Monday with ample work attire for the week and your bike on a rack. Commute via a combination of one or more methods—bike, car pool, or public transit—for the remainder of the week, until Friday evening, when you drive home.

Planning and Organizing

Considering all the identified potential solutions, possible pitfalls, and subsequent mitigation plans, the purpose of the next phase is to identify, document and organize the incremental steps required to achieve the agreed upon desired results and avoid potential pitfalls. Identify which of these steps can happen in parallel (concurrently), and which are in series (one task requiring completion before the next can

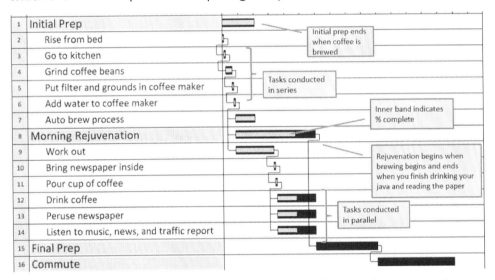

Figure 16: Graphical representation (Gantt chart) of the "get to work on time" process

start). The "get to work on time" example has tasks in series and parallel. First there are several serial tasks: rise from bed, go to the kitchen to start the coffee brewing, grind the beans, grab the filter, add grounds, add the water, and push start. Then there are a few parallel tasks—while the coffee is brewing, exercise for fifteen minutes—followed by more tasks in series: you grab the morning paper and pour a cup of coffee. Then, in parallel, you enjoy your coffee while perusing the newspaper and listening to music and the traffic report.

Once the major steps are identified, you need to determine who will own each step, when each step is due, and how much money, if any, is required to complete each step. You might also need to determine the number of expected hours per week each owner will spend on his or her task, and if any key contributors (helpers) are required to complete each task or subtask. (As the owner analyzes the expectations of each task, he or she may add subtasks that are required to complete the primary objective, some of which may require new team members.) Finally, the project leader and the owner of each task or subtask should agree on the metrics of success: how will they each know and agree the task has been completed successfully?

Figure 16, a Gantt chart, is a graphical representation of each significant step required to complete a project and is a helpful tool for planning and monitoring the progress of fairly simple to extremely intricate projects, though not necessary for those we conduct instinctively. One can imagine the complexity of a program for designing and erecting a skyscraper, for instance, and how keeping all those tasks organized in one's mind would likely be catastrophic. Gantt charts are elegant in their simplicity yet perceivable as complex. I've divided the "get to work on time" project into four phases: initial prep, morning rejuvenation, final prep, and commute. Each of these phases has several subtasks, though the subtasks for final prep and commute are not shown. The dark bar for each task shows the amount of time that is planned for or allotted to each task, while the inner, lighter bar represents the percentage complete for each task. In the example, initial prep and all its subtasks are 100 percent complete, whereas morning rejuvenation is 75 percent complete, and neither the final prep nor commute is started.

Getting It Done!

When you're satisfied that the plan is sound, it's time to execute! Execution requires each of the thinking modes to be successful. Continued organizational skills are required to coordinate activities, meetings, and data. Data analysis is required to determine results. Creative thinking is required to develop and refine solutions. Critical thinking is required to determine what may go wrong, and more creative thinking is required to mitigate risks and to solve or avoid problems. When monitoring a project, there are three major levers available to a project manager to adjust outcomes: cost, schedule, and performance. Once a baseline project plan is established, the team monitors progress toward its objectives relative to the cost, schedule and performance targets. Most leaders desire that all programs simultaneously, quickly and cost effectively improve performance. It is not uncommon for a team to feel pressure to improve on all three fronts (cost, schedule, and performance). While not impossible, simultaneous enhancement of all three metrics is not probable. It is possible, however, to improve on two fronts at any given time. For instance, if stakeholders are able to compromise on performance (accept lower performance), the team is likely to reduce both time and cost. If, on the other hand, stakeholders need to pull in the schedule, the team may have to compromise performance, cost, or both. Interestingly, a reduced schedule in scenario one leads to lower cost (fewer tasks are likely required to achieve lower performance), and in scenario two leads to increased costs (expedited fees and additional labor are required to fit the same number of tasks into less time).

Take Time to Smell the Roses

Finally, once you've completed your project, it's time for a celebration. Take time to smell the roses. If this is a solo project, treat yourself. If it is a team project, treat the team. Life is too short to pass over celebrations of successes, especially the small daily successes that are easily overlooked but just as easily enjoyed. Recall the example project of getting to work on time: "You tote the bagels, fruit, coffee, and your computer into the office, quickly arrange the conference room, release a deep sigh of relief, and then enjoy an exhilarating jolt of confidence just as your colleagues begin to arrive."

Recapping, the project management process falls into six major steps with several subsections:

1. Define: optimistic and analytical thinking (yellow and white hats)
   a. Purpose: why are you doing the project?
   b. Background information: reflect on experience and historical data.
   c. Expected outcomes: what do you need to achieve? By when?
2. Form a team: organizational and analytical thinking (blue and white hats)
   a. What skills are required to achieve your desired results?
   b. Estimate how much time you will require from each skill set and over what time period.
   c. Who has those skills and is available and willing?
3. Brainstorm: optimistic, creative, critical, and organizational thinking (yellow, green, black, and blue hats)
   a. How do you best achieve your desired results?
   b. What are possible or probable problems?
   c. How do you prevent problems before they occur?
4. Plan, organize, and identify next steps: organizational thinking (blue hat)
   a. What steps do you need to take in order to achieve your desired results and avoid pitfalls?
   b. Which steps can happen in parallel?
   c. Which steps must happen in series?
   d. Who will own each step?
      i. When will each step be completed?
      ii. How much of the owner's time is required for each step?
      iii. How much money is required?
      iv. Will the owner require additional help?

     e. How will you measure the success of each step (performance metrics)?
5. Execute, monitor, and steer (blue, white, green, black, and red hats)
     a. How will you track progress?
       i. Cost
       ii. Schedule
       iii. Performance
     b. Continually monitor results and adjust accordingly.
       i. Meet in person and/or on the phone, scheduled and/or ad hoc.
       ii. Identify and respond to risks.
6. Evaluate and celebrate. (White and Red)

Often we think of tools such as project planning as being reserved for our work lives, but we can become so much more effective by using and sharpening our tools in all phases and arenas of life. Think of a time you were in a life-changing situation outside of work, such as when selecting a college to attend, getting married, buying your first automobile or home, planning a remodel, or planning where to live in retirement. The process required to manage any of these larger projects is the same as that required to get ready for work in the morning, but as both complexity and risks rise, so does the need to plan. You may also find that when adding yet another project to the mix, such as getting married, your other obligations don't magically disappear miraculously creating free time for you to manage your plan to achieve eternally wedded bliss. No, life piles it on higher and deeper, challenging you to not only plan but set priorities and make choices regarding what you stop doing in order to take on another project.

Setting priorities among your projects is like placing them into different buckets. Think of your ongoing projects as either: **critical** (must have, can't do without), **important** (detrimental if not executed, but not fatal), or **optional** (few downsides if not executed). In addition to isolated benefit, we must also consider a project's level of difficulty, strategic importance, and expected benefit or value in relation to other objectives. Recall that the project-selection process is designed specifically to prioritize your projects relative to one another. Once you have selected your projects—what to work on and what not to work on—ranked them in importance, and created appropriate plans, you are ready to execute.

> **Efficiency is doing things right; effectiveness is doing the right things.**
> Peter Drucker

Execute: Work Together to Achieve Mutual Benefit

The execution phase corresponds to the 'do' phase in the See-Plan-Do-get process. A major component of fulfilling your high-level vision is creating a process that links your vision (how you see the future) to daily activities. In other words, you must work to achieve your vision, and your management process must connect the fifty-thousand-foot vision, whether personal or work related, to daily activities where the rubber actually meets the road (refer to Figure 17: Create a process that connects your fifty-thousand-foot view to daily activities. Live life focused on the important and not just the urgent.)

The highest-level view, the fifty-thousand-foot view (imagine flying in a supersonic jet far above the earth), is the desired end state. For your company, it may be becoming the world's best supplier of something or

> **A really great talent finds its happiness in execution.**
> Johann Wolfgang von Goethe

"refreshing the world." For your family, it may simply be becoming a family that is happily and regularly visited by friends, family, and loved ones. A family to whom even the grown children wish to visit on the holidays. Whatever the vision, it is meant to be inspiring, challenging and a beacon providing guidance in both good times and bad.

The next level, the forty-thousand-foot view, is also meant to endure over the life of the team or individual. Perhaps this level represents the inspirational missions of each major department or project team in your organization (e.g., "Our corporate mission is to create value for our shareholders, provide a great working environment for our team, and give back to our community"), or perhaps it represents the mission or vision of each of your household's family members. Recall each of my family members' individual aspirations to be "someone who values relationships; accepts responsibility; rejects passivity; contributes; leads courageously with consideration, passion, and integrity; and believes in grace and mercy."

Next comes the twenty- to forty-thousand-foot view. As your "plane" descends, the view becomes a bit clearer—more refined. Consequently, goals at this level should be better defined and more near term, spanning perhaps one to a few years. The following are examples of personal and business goals of varying scope and duration:

1. Complete high school with better than a 3.5 GPA while participating in the Associated Student Body government and at least one varsity sport in four years.
2. Complete bachelor and master of science degrees in biochemistry from 2015 through 2021, with a GPA greater than 3.8 and graduating in the top 10 percent of my class.
3. Get married. Plan a small, intimate wedding and get married nine months from today for a set budget of (enter your quantified budget number here).
4. Buy our first home within the next two years while maintaining a monthly debt-to-income ratio of less than 30 percent.
5. Increase revenue from sales of new products (introduced within the past eighteen months) by $1 million in 2015 (Figure 17).
6. Reduce the time required to execute payroll by 50 percent from 2014 to 2015.

As your "plane" continues its descent, the details of the landscape are clearer still: the five- to twenty-thousand-foot view represents one- to twelve-month deliverables or key milestones necessary to reach your longer-term goals.

1. Complete my fall semester in Advanced Placement (AP) Biology with an A-minus or better while fulfilling the Associated Student Body treasurer duties and participating in varsity gymnastics.

94

2. Complete my undergraduate research project and achieve an A on my undergraduate thesis.
3. Assign owners to each major wedding task and agree on due dates: find and book venue, schedule pastor, choose florist, choose bridesmaids, choose groomsmen, book entertainment, and so on.
4. Use a balloon-payment process to pay off student loans over next six months.
5. Close contract for a quarter-four deliverable of $180,000 with customer X (Figure 17).
6. Complete payroll-process value-stream mapping (mapping the process flow with the intent of removing wasteful steps, so only the steps that add value remain or at least the time spent on non-valued added work (reviewing and testing) is minimized) by the end of the first quarter.

Your plane lands, and the rubber meets the road. The runway is remarkably clear. Your luggage, exit aisle, and jetway exit are clear and represent near-term tasks (one to ninety days) each with a well-defined scope.

1. Read chapter one of the biology textbook and complete associated worksheet by Sunday.
2. Complete final thesis lab experiment by next Tuesday.
3. Call Mom this week to see if she can book Pastor Ron and choose florist by this Friday.
4. Add extra $75 to my student loan payment.
5. Confirm appointment with Tom of Company XYZ and book flights to finalize and sign contract (Figure 17).
6. Work with Serrena, the resident six-sigma black belt who is trained in the continuous improvement methodologies developed by Motorola and popularized by Jack Welch during his tenure as CEO of General Electric, to complete agenda for our value-stream mapping kaizen (continuous improvement effort to reduce waste).

50,000 foot view:
Company Vision
(Now & over life of company)

40,000 foot view:
Company (Team) mission
(Now & over life of company/team)

20–40,000 foot view:
Goals & Projects
(1 to 5 years)

5–20,000 foot view:
Deliverables & projects
(1 to 12 months)

On the ground: Where the rubber meets the road
Tasks: (1 to 90 days)

ABC Company

Our Vision: Enhance the lives of our customers, shareholders and community through a continuous supply of innovative and cost effective widgets...making life more enjoyable one day at a time.

ABC Corporate Team

Our mission is to create value for our shareholders, provide a great working atmosphere for our employees and provide value to the community

Increase Revenue: New Product Sales (+$1M) - On Target

Achieve $1.0M sales from products introduced < 18 months prior: $100k from Surefire, $500K from SpitFire, $400K from CoolFire

Deliverables

Title	Status	Start	Due	%	$
Q1 Revenue $280k	On Target	12/31/2014	3/31/2015	25	$1,000.00

+ Create Deliverable

Tasks

Title	Status	Start	Due	%	$
Close XYZ Q4 contract ($1.80k)	✓ Complete	12/31/2014	1/11/2015	10	$600.00

+ Create Task

Options

Figure 17: Create a process that connects your fifty-thousand-foot view to daily activities. Live life focused on the important and not just the urgent. Screenshots taken from Cloud Effective's Productivity Pro app, which cascades visions and missions to goals, projects, and tasks).

Continuity in execution is required to achieve sustainable excellence. A great idea without execution is worth no more than the back of the envelope or napkin it is written on. Another key is using an established process to ensure you are not constantly fighting fires. Work routinely on the nonurgent and important, keeping gas in the tank for crisis management. Encourage

> **I think having a great idea is vastly overrated. I know it sounds kind of crazy and counterintuitive. I don't think it matters what the idea is, almost. You need great execution.**
>
> Felix Dennis

your team to live a balanced life, spending time on what Stephen Covey refers to as quad-two activities: continuous improvement, self-renewal, and problem prevention. Thus, when important and urgent quad-one activities arise, you (and your team) will be ready, willing, and able to respond. Recall the JNJ versus BMY stock price comparison from 1999 to 2014. One can surmise that JNJ employees were more likely to have lived balanced lives leading up to the troubled 2000s than the BMY employees, who were likely to have spent an inordinate amount of time firefighting even when the stock prices were faring well—so that when trouble hit, the BMY employees might not have had enough gas in the tank to increase efforts even further. The side effect of prolonged firefighting is that you (and your team) are naturally worn-out from the stress of urgent firefighting; so do not naturally invest time in important but nonurgent fire prevention activities. Fires interrupt or completely stall progress toward innovative and preventative improvement objectives. They lead you and your team members to seek "escape" when not involved in firefighting. Alas, for most, the natural tendency when attempting to escape is not to work on that which is important. No, escaping is working on that which is not important and not urgent—spending too much time on e-mail, snail mail, voice mail, water-cooler talk, internet searches, meaningless "research," playing video games, too much time spent watching television, movies, or YouTube videos, spending too much time in poorly run meetings, and so on. The inevitable result—when "real" crises arise (as opposed to self-imposed crises due to lack of discipline and process)—is that there is nothing in the fuel tank: you and your team are crushed under the

The effectiveness of work increases according to geometric progression if there are no interruptions.

Andre Maurois

weight of the new emergency, which combines with all your smaller fires to overwhelm your forces. I have helped many a team to climb out of the trap of habitual firefighting, but not without hard work and commitment to change. If you are constantly fighting fire and wish to become more productive—something needs to change. Put first things first, turn to your team to seek improvement (refer to figures 8 and 9).

Forming to Performing

By setting and adhering to priorities, a team develops the discipline to do the right things and say no to the wrong things. In other words, healthy guidelines (boundaries) of engagement are established. This is not hierarchical discipline but discipline that exists at the core of your culture—self-discipline fueled by self-motivation. How does this happen?

To reiterate, first get the right people on the bus. Second, include them in the planning to achieve buy-in. I have read and heard much about how to motivate others, but I believe people are basically born with core motivations and then learn both the good and bad habits associated with those innate motivations. Consequently, the best way to assemble a motivated team is to find self-motivated people (people focused on the positive behaviors associated with their core motivation) and do nothing to demotivate them (do nothing to prompt them to revert to the poor behaviors associated with their core motivation). As you form the team, determine which types of motivations you require and in which positions. Find people who have a history of behaviors that indicate a strong presence of the necessary skills and bring them on board. Do you need drivers who are motivated to get things done? Do you need leaders who are motivated to help others succeed? Do you require thinkers to create calm and add logic in the midst of frenzied activity? Do you need articulate and persuasive leaders to guide, sell, teach, or train? Find the right people to fill these needs. This is a stage Jim Collins refers to as "first who" in his book *Good to Great.*

As the team takes form, members' initial behaviors are driven by a desire to be accepted, and thus, the early stages are relatively free of conflict and controversy. Team members are getting to know one another, becoming familiar with thought and behavioral patterns, and thus are often on their best behavior.

Soon the team begins to develop an understanding of its basic purpose—what the members have been brought together to deliver. Perhaps they are analyzing background information and discussing expected outcomes. Each member may be highly motivated, but each is likely motivated differently. These varied motivations combined with differing experiences can lead to disparate interpretations of the stated objective. Soon it becomes clear that a deeper (more unified) understanding of the desired results is required. The team begins to brainstorm options, some offering optimistic views of potential outcomes (yellow hat), and others countering with critical assessments (black hat).

When optimism encounters criticism, the first seeds of conflict are sown. Conflict begins to grow, and the team enters a stage coined "storming" by Bruce Tuckman in his team-development model: forming, storming, norming, and performing. The team strives to determine how it will best achieve the desired outcomes and fulfill its purpose. The members attempt to agree on potential obstacles and appropriate preventative actions, but they often find agreement is elusive at best. They begin to resist simple tasks and bicker even while agreeing on their fundamental purpose. They may begin to question the leaders who chartered the project. Some may strive to establish unrealistic goals, and the storming continues. So much negative energy is spent on team misalignment and personnel issues that little progress is made during this stage in a team's life cycle.

Fortunately, we have already covered the many requirements of successful relationships, which are of course necessary for successful teamwork (see "Manage Thought" in *VerAegis—Relationships*). Team leaders must help team members build trust by demonstrating how to treat one another with consideration while pursuing the "technical" path that individual expertise demands for success. Mentors and/or coaches must facilitate parallel thinking processes and nurture the maturity in team members to seek mutual benefit. Soon the team will leave much or all of the storming behind, instead beginning to develop healthy working patterns (the courage to use their expertise to make progress but the consideration to do so in a manner that allows teammates to simultaneously excel by also applying their particular expertise) and seeking a potential path to synergy.

Armed with a well-understood charter, high-level objectives, and improved pride of ownership, the team begins to refine plans, even becoming excited about different options and opportunities. The team dynamics improve as members settle into their roles, and either a formal or informal structure begins to develop. To be most effective, people who most need to work together should be on the same subteam, and reporting structures and responsibilities must be aligned to enable parallel rather than conflicting thought processes. Likewise, business systems must be established so that information flows to those who need it first to make decisions. Norms of performance and metrics of success are now established, perhaps with clear rewards determined in advance. The team determines if additional training or skill sets are necessary and proceeds accordingly. With an effective structure, the right processes, an effective reward system, and clearly defined ownership and success criteria, the team begins to perform well. When thus empowered, it may be a while before team members return to the storming phase.

I have found that many confuse the meaning of empowerment with the meaning of entitlement. Empowerment is not about giving something to someone who may not deserve the honor. Rather, empowerment is linked to merit. It is achieving effectiveness through the correct balance of capability, authority, and responsibility (CAR), where capability is a combination of the necessary character traits and sufficient or exceptional competence to deliver the desired results—over and over again. Competence, in turn, is a combination of knowledge (know-what: facts and information gained through experience and education) and skill (know-how: physical and mental dexterity gained through experience and training). Responsibility is the duty or task one is required to perform. Authority is the power to direct resources and make decisions.

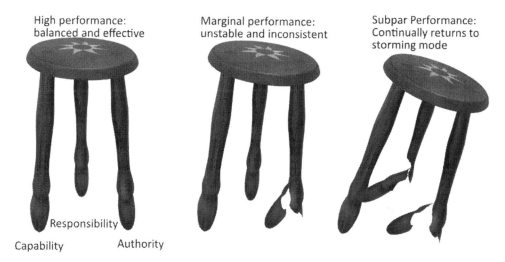

High performance: balanced and effective

Marginal performance: unstable and inconsistent

Subpar Performance: Continually returns to storming mode

Responsibility

Capability

Authority

Figure 18: Balanced and effective empowerment is possible only when capability, responsibility, and authority are balanced. Teams will never reach the performing mode or will continually return to storming when inappropriately empowered.

A person or team is appropriately empowered when the capability to perform a given duty is balanced with the

Nearly all men can stand adversity, but if you want to test a man's character, give him power.

Abraham Lincoln

101

magnitudes of authority (the power to direct resources and make decisions) and responsibility (job function or duties). A shortfall in one or two of the three components of empowerment results in unstable situations of micromanagement or abandonment. (Figure 18)

A person or team with higher levels of responsibility and authority than merited by capability is overempowered. That person or team will struggle and possibly feel abandoned, likely returning frequently to the storming stage. An overempowered person may be the product of the "Peter principle," meaning he or she was promoted until landing in a position wherein success was near impossible. This person is now underperforming and likely in the lower 10 percent of the organization or team. In order to succeed, this underperformer needs to be trained if the deficient skill is easily learned, or else he or she must find a more suitable position within or outside of the team if the skill set is more elusive. In the best-case scenario, the team and the underperformer are in agreement and move in concert to resolve the situation. The best way to avoid becoming victim to the Peter Principle is by clearly performing at the necessary level prior to being promoted into the position.

A highly capable person or team with a challenging position or project, but without the authority to direct the necessary resources and make decisions, will feel underempowered and micromanaged. The person's supervisor or team champion must quickly align this person's responsibility and authority with capability to prevent the likely transition from feeling underempowered to feeling completely disenchanted. This person should be nurtured as part of what Jack Welch calls the "vital 70" (70 percent of the people in any organization are vital to sustained success) or "top 20" (20 percent of the organization are responsible and capable to take the team to the next level providing sustained competitive advantage).

Similarly, a highly capable person or team with the authority to direct resources and make decisions, but without adequate tasks, duties, or projects (i.e., responsibility), will feel underutilized and underempowered. If this situation is not easily resolved, the team or organization may have bigger problems, because the solution is simply to find a challenging position and nurture him or her as part of the "vital 70" or "top 20." Note that if you find yourself in a company where a challenging position is not available, you should find such a position outside the workplace, either in a new job or as a volunteer; otherwise you will feel that you are not contributing, and your life will become out of balance.

Stephen Covey defined levels of empowerment from low to high in the following terms: wait until you are told what to do, ask for instructions, bring recommendations, do it and report immediately, do it and report routinely, and do it and report disposition. In other words, if you have just been hired to install high-pressured tanks of toxics gases, you will need to be trained before proceeding. Rather than telling you to just do it and report back, you are told to wait until you have been thoroughly trained and certified before you proceed. Once you have successfully installed several toxic-gas canisters, you are likely told to ask for instructions if you notice any deviations. As your expertise increases, you begin to make recommendations when deviations appear. Perhaps with continued training and experience, you become the supervisor of a small team and now just provide routine reports or report disposition when a job is completed.

High-performing families, teams and organizations function as cohesive units, executing, monitoring, and steering activities and results. They continually seek and achieve appropriate empowerment, progressing through the levels of empowerment as experience and capabilities are improved. Processes are employed but not at the expense of instincts and expertise. Such teams are alert and continually set goals and monitor results. They track cost, schedule, and performance. Results are monitored against a backdrop of SMART goals. Information flows quickly to those who need it to make decisions. Meetings are effective, whether in person, on the phone, scheduled, or ad hoc, and are held to move forward rather than cover your tracks.

SMART Goals

SMART is a helpful acronym used to remind us the components of a well-thought-out goal (Figure 19). There is a much higher probability of achieving a goal that is well thought-out and clearly articulated. Accordingly, SMART goals are results-driven planning statements that describe and quantify desired outcomes that individuals or teams are responsible to deliver. In other words, SMART goals are statements of important and measurable outcomes (or future destinations) that, when accomplished, will ensure the attainment of an individual's, family's, team's, or organization's highest priorities. SMART goals do not form a "wish list" but should stretch the organization in order to provide a challenging and exciting environment in which members are encouraged to excel.

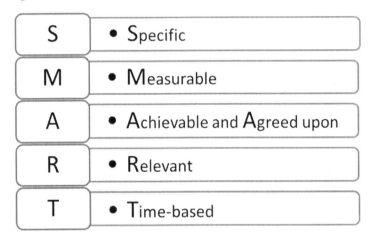

S	• Specific
M	• Measurable
A	• Achievable and Agreed upon
R	• Relevant
T	• Time-based

Figure 19: SMART goals are key to an effective organization that routinely obtains desired outcomes.

Specific

At home or at work, goals should be results oriented rather than action oriented. A specific, clearly articulated goal has a much greater chance of being accomplished than a general goal. To set a specific goal, you must answer six *W* questions:

- *What?* Document the desired outcome.
- *Why?* Identify specific reasons for accomplishing the goal.
- *Who?* Assign ownership. Who is the owner, and who is a key contributor? Who is the customer?
- *When?* Establish a time frame.
- *Where?* Identify where you will execute the plan to where the results (products or services) are to be delivered.
- *Which?* Identify which guidelines, requirements, and constraints are necessary.

By answering these questions, we determine what we are specifically responsible for delivering. As an example, a general action-oriented goal may be written as "work out regularly to get in shape." But a more specific goal is articulated, as in "join a health club and work out three days a week for thirty to forty-five minutes each day on Monday, Wednesday, and Friday, thus reducing my waistline by one inch and losing fifteen pounds over the next six months."

Measurable

Establish concrete, quantifiable criteria for measuring progress toward the attainment of each goal you set. If the goal is not measurable, it will be difficult to ascertain whether adequate progress toward successful completion is being made. With measurement of progress, however, comes the ability to react, which in turn significantly improves the chances of delivering desired results. Criteria for success should be stated in terms of quantity, quality, or timeliness.

To determine if your goal is measurable, ask questions such as the following:

- How much?
- How many?
- To what extent?
- How will I know when it is accomplished?
- Who cares and why?

- Is schedule important?

Through this process, you will also answer the question "what standards will be used to measure success?" In the previous "get in shape" example, three metrics of success were noted: weight, schedule, and ultimately the waistline measurement.

Achievable and Agreed Upon

To be achievable, a goal must represent an objective toward which you are both willing and able to work within current personal and/or organizational constraints. "Achievable" does not mean or imply that goals should be easy. In fact, an achievable goal can (and sometimes should) stretch both the individual and the organization. Each goal should represent substantial progress; some should represent extraordinary progress. It might seem counterintuitive, but a difficult goal that "stretches" an individual's or a team's capabilities sometimes seems more readily achievable than a comparably simple goal because the "stretch goal" exerts relatively high motivational force. Perhaps some of your greatest accomplishments actually seemed relatively easy—simply because they were labors of love.

Finally, even when we strive for substantial progress, we will not always succeed, and a goal that can no longer be achieved should be altered or abandoned.

To determine if a goal is achievable, one should ask (and honestly answer) the following questions:

- Is it possible to accomplish the goal in the established time frame and with other known constraints?
- Are the trade-offs between cost, schedule, and performance well understood? Which of these three levers is the highest priority?
- How is this goal best accomplished?
- Have I (we) overlooked opportunities to deliver these or better results?

106

- Do I (we) have the necessary resources and skills to accomplish this within other known constraints?
- Is this goal a stretch, but still within the realm of possibility?

The buy-in process is an essential element of goal execution. When attainment of one's goals requires assistance (as they so often do), it is important to identify interdependencies to ensure alignment with other goal owners. Without alignment and agreement among key stakeholders, you will have only an awfully limited chance to deliver mutually beneficial desired results. Thus, the goal-setting process should ensure that interested parties have a chance to buy into the goal definition as well as its deliverables. Buy-in, in turn, leads to more willingness to expend efforts toward achieving the goal (recall that lack of buy-in is a common obstacle to effective goal management). Agreement among all the stakeholders will facilitate a successful engagement and decrease the tendency to "storm" over differences and unmet expectations (reduce emotional debt).

- Each goal should be set by or in concert with the person or team responsible for its achievement.
- The team's leadership—and when appropriate, key stakeholders—should agree that the goal is important and that appropriate time and resources will be allocated to its successful completion.

Relevant

Simply stated, relevant goals are goals that matter to you and others. Each goal adopted should be one that moves the team or individual toward the achievement of its higher-level objectives. Ultimately, goals should be consistent with the fifty-thousand-foot view—with the mission and vision of the individual, family, team or organization.

Affirmative answers to the following questions will help to determine the relevancy of a goal:

- Does this goal seem important, relative to other goals?

- Will accomplishment of the desired results move us toward our desired vision of the future?
- Is this the right time?
- Am I the right person?
- Is this goal free from conflict with your other priorities?
- Is this goal free from conflict with other family, team or organizational goals?
- Is this effort receiving the necessary resources?
- Are others relying on the successful outcome of this goal?
- Are others invested, willing to help, and willing to review progress?

If one cannot answer yes to most of these questions, the goal should be reevaluated and realigned, or perhaps even abandoned. Recall that successful individuals and organizations need to be adept at learning when to say no.

Time-Based

For a goal to be truly SMART, there must be an agreed-upon timetable that incorporates regular, structured reviews of progress toward the goal. This schedule must contain more than just a simple start date and completion date; there should also be interim deliverables and checkpoints. By having a timeline, you ensure momentum and focus. Intermediate benchmarks provide both opportunities to correct your course, if necessary, and to celebrate short-term successes.

Ask yourself, "What is the timeline for completion of the goal?" Break the project into shorter terms associated with incremental milestones; for instance, add a quarterly deliverable for a year-long project, and include more details in the execution plans:

- Use Gantt charts (Figure 16) to manage critical path actions (actions which are deemed critical to the timeline in which you are able to deliver the desired results), and verify that near-term tasks and milestones are consistent with longer-term goals.

- Use action boards to deliver milestones for each of your programs, ideally with alerts and regular reviews to remind you and other team members of pending due dates.
- Prevent unrelated and irrelevant tasks or actions from becoming the focus of your attention, and don't allow tactical minutiae fill your calendar. Prior to beginning your week, review long term goals and plans, then allocate time on your calendar to address your most important goals, associated deliverables and tasks.

Teamwork and Conflict

Imagine that your team is performing well. Goals are established, and tasks are being checked off one after another. Business is booming. All is good, correct? Not so fast. Unfortunately, high-performing teams do not indefinitely maintain high levels of performance. They return time and again to storming, which then requires another "norming" phase before they return once again to performing.

Performing➔Storming➔Norming➔Performing

The cycle continues.

There are many dynamics that could cause the return to storming, but in my experience, four causes are most prevalent, and each leads to missed expectations. Missed expectations lead to storming:

- Inconsistent or constantly changing priorities
- Poor risk-management and problem-solving processes
- Poorly managed new opportunities that spread teams too thin
- Poorly managed innovation (e.g., new product or process development)

At times, fluctuations in company-wide (or family) dynamics drive broad changes that in turn negatively impacts effectiveness and focus on pre-existing priorities. For example, as companies grow (especially during the transition from small to medium size), systems and processes that once worked may no longer function effectively. Individuals who knew the processes inside and out perhaps did not document them, nor did they foresee how difficult it would be to scale—risks were unforeseen, and problems unresolved. Not surprisingly, the same transition occurs in a marriage. The relationship processes for newlyweds without children differ significantly from those required as the family grows. Sleep deprived parents often do not spend enough time aligning expectations which leads to storming and tumultuous rides on the crazy cycle (see *VerAegis—Relationships*)

In both families and business, growth and new opportunities mean that work expands. More and more effort is diverted to running the company rather than developing products or services and generating revenue. In families, more effort is diverted to supporting the family rather than developing relationships and communication skills. These new dynamics drive changes to individual priorities that, when not aligned (i.e., agreed upon and orchestrated), begin to rip relationships apart. Growing families, teams, and organizations often feel helpless and continually return to storming mode. For example, newly hired operations experts find themselves squarely in conflict with those who have moved the company or team to where it is today. Sleep deprived parents—once loving husbands and respectful wives are spread thin, each blaming the other for not delivering results for which the expectations were never aligned. At home and at work, when desired results and priorities are not agreed upon, effectiveness and success are elusive.

When Priorities Collide

When faced with conflicting priorities and misaligned expectations, it is important to recognize some of the key behaviors (triggers) in ourselves and others that move us, our families, teams, and entire organizations from high performance (assertive and proactive) to lower performance (storming—reactive, anger prone, and conflict ridden). Recognition is the prerequisite to prevention. Left unchecked, some team members begin to respond aggressively to situations. The resulting environment of low openness and low consideration causes a precipitous decline in performance, negatively impacting the ability to deliver desired results, which in turn causes further damage to relationships; it's the crazy cycle of teams and families. When confidence erodes, the overall vision seems to become a joke or distant memory, and the team begins to lose sight of its objectives.

> **You have to feel confident. If you don't, then you're going to be hesitant and defensive, and there'll be a lot of things working against you.**
>
> Clint Eastwood

Rewriting Hrand Saxenian's definition of emotional maturity to reflect team dynamics yields the following: **the current level of a family's or team's emotional maturity is indicated by the extent to which members express feelings and convictions in balance with consideration for the abilities, thoughts, and feelings of others, without being threatened by the expression of either one's own or others' ideas or feelings.** In other words, the most effective families and teams operate openly, each member wielding the courage to embrace his or her expertise and convictions while simultaneously maintaining the consideration to let others do the same—ever vigilant to signs that they might be slipping from the high-performance quadrant to lower-performing quadrants (Figure 20).

Let us consider a few priority-alignment scenarios in a high-performing team that is on the verge of either moving to the next level or slipping into full-blown storming.

The situation is as follows: Toni, VP of sales, and her team have identified a great opportunity, perhaps the best to date for their young company. She is optimistic, and as she prepares for her last meeting of the day, she thinks momentarily of her evening plans: she will stop on the way home to pick up a few last-minute items to prepare for a small party with a few of her closest friends. Tom, VP of engineering, is anxious, perhaps even pessimistic. Tom's team is overburdened, and

111

he fears Toni intends to introduce yet another project without a cancellation or change of urgency to existing projects. As of late, Tom's

		Level of consideration	
		Low consideration: prideful and contemptuous	High consideration: humble and respectful
Level of courage	High courage: confident and engaging	Focused primarily on most important personal priorities with little concern or consideration for balance or input regarding others' priorities **Causes of low consideration:** • Pride and the need to be right. • Reactive toward team or family members who wait for a priority to hit a level of urgency prior to really digging in—due to negligence or just for the thrill of the firefight! • At times, inconsiderate responses are poor reactions to closed, misleading communication. The perceived affront (such as a hidden agenda) combined with a pessimistic view that he or she is not being taken seriously, may result in aggressive rather than assertive behavior.	Tackles high priorities before they become urgent with consideration for the self and the needs of others, leaving "gas in the tank" should an urgent situation arise, and views differences as opportunities for synergy • Open-minded, listens to understand • Openhearted, cares about others • Courageous, does not abandon beliefs and convictions • Integrity: Does what is right even when no one is looking This high-performing quadrant is where we all should strive to operate. We should be aware of situations and behaviors in others that trigger the worst in us and move us to the lower-performing quadrants.
	Low courage: insecure and closed	Desires alignment but may choose to avoid setting clear priorities due to the following: • Fear of being "boxed in" and missing the "next big thing" • Conflict avoidance—unwilling to work through alignment issues that arise from disagreement • A combination of pride, fear, and lack of the humility required to put self aside and engage openly May agree to a course of action without the intention to follow through. When negatively motivated (especially by aggressive behavior), likely will not inform others that they are not working on the agreement until it is too late	Desires alignment but at times too willing to accept others' priorities at the expense of one's own priorities and the ability to follow through on other commitments Hates to say no, even if the goal or objective is not relevant • May move from an engaging to closed style of communication when confronted with unkind behavior • Suppressed angst may build up over time, and if not dealt with in a healthy fashion, may lead to "explosions." • Inability to say no can lead to being spread too thin; goals may suffer and in turn create conflicts in personal or work relationships.

Figure 20: Remaining in or returning quickly to the upper right (most mature) quadrant is vital to high performance in individuals, teams, and entire organizations.

projects CoolFire and HipFire, two of his three top priorities, have been riddled with technical difficulties that have caused serious delays and now sales (Toni) is meeting to pitch yet another proposal to launch project SureFire.

Toni initiates interaction assertively, confidently presenting the opportunity to Tom. Tom privately disagrees with the proposal from the moment she begins and is barely able to concentrate as he ponders ways to shoot her down and end the meeting. Soon his critical (black-hat) thinking spills over. He is certainly open but lashes out without consideration for Toni or her team, who sit quietly in shock. Tom is subconsciously pessimistic that he will be taken seriously without becoming boisterous, and he wants to show Toni the light! He needs her to understand that taking on another project before at least one existing project is completed is not only inadvisable but downright irresponsible. Tom's ire grows. He becomes openly aggressive in false hopes of forcing agreement. Tom is in the upper left quadrant—high levels of courage but low levels of consideration.

Tom's inconsiderate, forceful approach is a potential trigger for Toni. Toni has a few options: she can back down and let her project die, hurting herself, her team, her customer, and the company she is trying to help grow; she can close up and avoid conflict by passively agreeing with Tom, then work behind the scenes to gain Kevin's (the CEO's) support for her project; she can go toe-to-toe with Tom, meeting his inconsiderate attitude head-on; or she can remain confident and considerate, outlining the opportunity and learning as much as she can from Tom so that she understands and is able to address each of his objections.

In the scenario where Toni backs down to Tom's aggression, Toni's weakness is lack of courage. When negatively motivated by inconsiderate behavior, she opts to disengage. Subconsciously pessimistic that she will be taken seriously if open and honest, Toni may suppress her anxiety and continue to seek understanding if she clings to high levels of consideration. But without courage, she ultimately capitulates, allowing Tom to have his way. She settles for a loss and fails to pursue this great opportunity. By conceding, Toni is able to quiet Tom, and though she feels walked on, she thinks of herself as a noble martyr. She pauses a moment before she leaves for the day and wishes she could have done better.

In the scenario where Toni lacks both courage and consideration, she responds poorly to Tom's aggressive behavior by closing up but is covertly unkind and inconsiderate. She agrees when face-to-face to cancel the project in order to end the immediate conflict. However, she has no intention of letting her project die, and she plans to force the project through by gaining approval from Kevin (the CEO and mutual boss) without seeking to understand the obstacles faced by Tom and his team. Toni has fallen to low levels of both courage and consideration (the lower left quadrant). She leaves the meeting feeling indignant, thinking, "I'll show Tom for treating me like that." She feels contempt, though she does not perceive herself as inconsiderate because she did not outwardly display her anger (as did Tom). Nonetheless, she shudders slightly at the thought of going behind Tom's back to get the problem solved. She pauses for a moment and wishes she could have done better.

In both cases, Tom convinces himself his behavior was justified: "I got my way, so the end justifies the means." For a moment, he feels bad about responding aggressively, and he wishes quietly that he could have done better, but he simply couldn't risk exposing his already overburdened team to yet another project.

If, in another scenario, Toni responds to Tom's initial inconsiderate rebuff with courage, but without consideration for his concerns—she too becomes aggressive in false hopes of forcing agreement. At this point, neither party is seeking to understand. Toni's in-kind inconsiderate, forceful response is a likely trigger for Tom to escalate. Tom realizes deep down that there is a better way, but he is pessimistic that he will be heard without further escalation. He bites. Not to be swayed, Toni decides to battle it out. They go toe-to-toe, voices are raised, and unkind words fly. All others in the meeting shut down. A few discreetly leave. In the past, when Toni and Tom went at it, they would often become so angry that one or both would storm out of the room, but today the stakes are too high, and neither will back down.

Tom looks Toni in the eyes as he leans across the table and shouts, "I understand you are excited and feel this product will be the best thing since sliced bread, but something has to give!" Exasperated, he drops into his chair. "Why can't you see we are on the verge of failing to deliver on two of your other 'biggest and best' projects? We can't take on more without making adjustments!"

Toni sees Tom's emotions begin to settle. Calming herself, she returns to her chair. "Tom, I do recognize that something has to change. We cannot continue doing what we have been doing and expect different results, which is why I am here. I and my team want to work with you and your team to plan a solution. If we work together to present a plan next week to the customer, I am confident they will provide development funding so that we can bring in more resources. I am asking for some of your time to determine what resources are necessary to recover your existing projects and take on this program as well."

Tom feels understood. He lowers his defenses completely and agrees to work with Toni. They each feel justified as they think, "We found a solution, so the end justifies the means," but deeper down, they each regret their unkind response to anger and wish they could have done better. Why did it take so long for them to be assertive and act with a balance of courage and kindness?

Take note: the subconscious response to a negative motivation requires a conscious countermeasure (at least until a new habit is formed). There are three conditions that must be met in order for the countermeasure to be effective and thus prevent a "typical" response triggered by the subconscious mind:

1. Recognition of the trigger

2. Moment of pause to collect your thoughts (to recall your plan and in order to be slow in your response to anger)
3. A plan conceived in advance. The plan should consist of a few easy steps that help you remain in balance, displaying high levels of courage balanced with consideration. This will require proactivity, openness, humility, respect, a willingness to really understand the other's position, and dedication to achieving a win for both parties. The best-case scenario is that you work out a plan with your partner or colleague in advance by asking, "When [the situation] happens, what would you like for me to say to you that will not upset you but will alert you to the fact that I am becoming upset, and that we need to switch gears to prevent escalation?"

Build upon the following sample plan:

1. My mind-set: I will be pragmatically optimistic that I can courageously achieve my desired outcome without becoming unkind or inconsiderate.
2. I will listen with the intent to understand others' positions, convictions, and worries, not so that I can argue but in order to restate their position in my own words until they are satisfied that I understand their needs. I will remember that understanding does not mean agreeing. Understanding is the first step to lowering barriers so that reconciliation and resolution can be achieved.
3. I will invite them to use collaborative thinking.
   a. I will use my plan (blue hat): when emotions escalate, I will empathically mirror feelings and invite them to share their feelings when we are engaged in emotional and intuitive (red-hat) thinking. I will use the predetermined statement we have developed together if available.

b. I will invoke pragmatically optimistic (yellow-hat) thinking to find the good in their proposal.

c. Next we will use analytical (white-hat) thinking to present relevant data and information that may illuminate alternative paths or support the existing proposal.

d. Together we will invoke critical (black-hat) thinking to identify potential pitfalls and problems.

e. Next we will invoke creative (green-hat) thinking to brainstorm creative solutions.

f. We will return to blue-hat thinking to document outcomes and next steps.

g. We will end by sharing our intuitive responses to the outcomes and next steps to determine how we each feel about the new proposal. Have we realized any new insights or gut responses? What do our instincts say?

This same type of process may be applied to any type of conflict, not just differences in priorities. It is simple, but it is not easy. It requires practice and perseverance. You may do well once and fail the next time under the same or different circumstances. You may succeed with one person but fail in your attempts with another. Don't despair. You need to reassess your plan, consider your delivery, try again, evaluate the results, and continue the cycle until your responses are more proactive than reactive.

This approach is similar to that of a martial artist who may practice hundreds or even thousands of self-defense moves against various attacks. The martial artist practices over and over again until the moves are second nature, so that when faced with an attack, he or she responds, neutralizes the assault, positions himself or herself for advantage, and resolves the conflict. Perhaps that's not quite a win-win, but the concept of having a premeditated plan of action for each type of attack mimics our need for a plan for each of the strong negative motivators we know we will face. Who pushes your buttons?

How do they push your buttons? How do you typically respond? Will you have a plan next time so that you stand up for your abilities, feelings, and convictions while remaining kind and considerate? Do you and this person share a mutual desire to collaborate and to develop a plan?

Recall Toni's fourth option in responding to Tom's aggressive approach: remain confident and considerate, outlining the opportunity and learning as much as she can from Tom so that she understands and is able to address each of his objections. In each of the scenarios we reviewed, Toni was initially optimistically pragmatic, but she was not resolved to remain assertive in the face of negative triggers. Tom started in a bad place and disagreed with Toni's proposal from the outset. They each caved to their inherent weaknesses and were subconsciously pessimistic that they could assertively achieve their desired results. In each of the prior scenarios, Toni either became closed off or openly aggressive. Toni's lack of engagement or open aggression were both triggers to Tom, and he reacted poorly by choosing to escalate rather than seeking to understand.

If instead Toni and Tom had plans in place and were each resolved to achieve desired outcomes without becoming inconsiderate, they would have avoided angst and pain for themselves and their teams. After a few disagreements, Toni and Tom were able to work together on their new plan. For the most part, they now listen with the intent to understand in order to restate in their own words the other's position until they each feel understood. They initiate and subscribe to collaborative (parallel) thinking and organize their interaction by moving fluidly through the various modes of thought. Initially they struggled with mutually respectful engagements and became frustrated. At times they almost gave in to temptations to disengage or to become aggressive, but one or the other was always able to avoid the temptation and break the cycle. They agreed on a few scripted statements to alert each other of potentially unhealthy conflict, such as, "Hey, let's save the valuable black-hat thinking for later." Slowly the pessimistic, defensive posture faded as one or the other began to demonstrate clear understanding. They now realize that the key to breaking the cycle of immature responses to anger is truly caring enough to seek and achieve understanding, without fearing that the act of understanding will be misconstrued as agreement.

As a result, their teams have aligned priorities. Process-improvement projects are running well. The organization is committed to continuous improvement. New product development is proceeding well, and the organization is poised for renewed growth. But what might happen when a new "idea guy" (or gal) is added to the team? New ideas lead to new opportunities, new opportunities to new projects, and new projects to new priorities—and potentially to new conflicts. Problems begin to surface and seem to go unresolved. All of a sudden, the team is thrown back into storming as dissension rises and priorities are no longer aligned. Team members are once again spread thin. The attitude of cooperation is threatened. In fact, a new attitude of distrust surfaces, inhibiting progress. What next steps are required to invoke an *organizational* attitude adjustment?

Recall the conflict between Toni and Tom. Toni wanted Tom to change priorities; Tom was frustrated and did not want to leave projects CoolFire and HipFire in the lurch for the promise of SureFire. Raj, VP of operations; Kevin, CEO; and Theresa, VP of finance and accounting, all had their own opinions and plans regarding the situation. They each were impressed by Toni and Tom ultimately resolving differences and working so well together. They collectively sought to understand Toni and Tom's transformation in hopes that the same process could help the larger organization. It did not take long for the team to realize that Toni and Tom had created a framework of engagement, and from there it became apparent that more teamwork and processes were required to facilitate additional growth. The team quickly agreed to develop processes to evaluate new opportunities in conjunction with existing projects, to identify and mitigate risks and problems, and to manage new product and process development. Members were of the same mind regarding executive sponsorship and also agreed to a "crawl, walk, and then run" process so that they could first take baby steps and then grow and improve the processes as the company matured.

Toni, Tom, and Theresa tackled the new-opportunity-review process. Raj and Kevin tackled problem solving and risk mitigation. They all opted to team up for the NPI (New Product Innovation or Introduction) process.

New-Opportunity-Review

Since their teams had returned to storming mode after hiring the new "idea guy," Toni and Tom prioritized development of an improved process to manage new ideas and opportunities. Because new ideas often mean new products, Toni and Tom realized that new-opportunity reviews could function as an early stage step in a NPI process and so structured the objectives accordingly:

1. When possible, address each opportunity with existing, qualified products.
2. If existing products do not meet the requirements, strive to address opportunities by using a new combination of existing platforms.
3. Next, strive to address opportunities by modifying one or more existing platforms.
4. Last, address opportunities by developing new platforms.

Guidelines were quickly set in place. They easily agreed that all new opportunities meeting the first objective would be owned by sales and operations, only requiring additional approval if the pricing was outside of standards or in the event of unforeseen spending requirements. No development resources were required. Opportunities that fell into objectives two, three, or four would meanwhile serve as the funnels to the new product-development procedure (see "New Product or Process Introduction").

In order to avoid the conflict that had plagued their earlier relationship, Toni and Tom agreed to structure the meeting in a way that would encourage parallel thinking. The opportunity would be first presented by sales or product-line marketing using optimistic (yellow-hat) thinking to define the value of the opportunity. The meeting's blue-hat facilitator, using brainstorming rules, would ensure critical (black-hat) thinking was saved for later by emphasizing the importance of covering the benefits first so that everyone would be equally aware of the potential upsides. Toni and Tom agreed that the purpose of sharing the upsides first was to create an attitude of excitement and buy-in prior to exposing potential problems using the black hat. By being presented with the upsides first, the team members would be less likely to feel discouraged by problems and would later be motivated by the upsides to identify potential obstacles instead with the mind-set of finding better solutions.

With the upsides vetted, the team would progress to critical thinking using the black hat, identifying potential problems, shortcomings, and risks. If the black hat were covered too soon, the team might feel overwhelmed by problems, but with the upsides established and the mind-set in place that identification leads to prevention, the downsides could be thoroughly explored while remaining mindful that some problems' solutions would require too much time or money to be justified.

Following the black hat, the team would use creative thinking (the green hat) to brainstorm. Members would outline potential solutions for meeting product or process requirements to achieve the benefits identified in the yellow-hat session. Likewise, they would outline plans to mitigate the identified risks from the black-hat session (e.g., design issues, programming issues, and operational deployment issues) and lead to successful deployment should the project receive a thumbs-up.

They agreed to next use analytical white-hat thinking to evaluate the data gathered to date and determine whether the proposal held water financially. They would answer the questions "can we do this?" and, perhaps more importantly, "should we do this?" Estimated cost would be evaluated based on green-, black-, and yellow-hat sessions. What does the data suggest about the likelihood of market fruition, the probability of meeting product performance standards and achieving profitability (proven, highly likely, good chance, even chance, hit or miss, long shot, etc.)? How many projects were ongoing? Did they have underutilized resources? Would the opportunity potentially support the addition of new resources? The team next would evaluate the return on investment, compare to other projects and make a determination.

Using the blue and white hats, the team would rate and rank each project relative to ongoing projects using a project-selection matrix (see "Plan and Prioritize"). Finally, the team would review the outcome for completeness and then solicit intuitive and instinctive (red-hat) thinking. Did they feel good about the process and the outcome? Did the risks and rewards appear to be in balance? Did they think this would be a successful, profitable, and fulfilling project? If satisfied with the analysis, the team would employ the white hat to recommend the next step: go, hold, or evaluate (Figure 14).

The new-opportunity review (NOR) agenda can be recapped as followed:

1. Optimistic thinking (yellow hat): Present the opportunity.
2. Critical thinking (black hat): Identify potential problems. Define consequences if the project goes extremely awry.
3. Creative thinking (green hat): Invent solutions for potential problems.
4. Analytical thinking (white hat): Can we do this? Should we do this?
5. Organizational thinking (blue hat): Organize data into a project-selection matrix and graph.

6. Intuitive and instinctive thinking (red hat): How do you feel about the decision? What does your gut (instinct) say about the likelihood of success?
7. Analytical and organizational thinking (white and blue hats): Place projects into the categories of go, hold, or evaluate.

Theresa created a few easy-to-use financial tools, and the team was ready to present the process to Kevin's staff. Upon review, the process was implemented with only one minor change: Raj suggested that continuous improvement opportunities be included in the same matrix, since many of the resources were shared.

A Horse by Any Other Name: Seven Steps, DMAIC, 8D, and Five Whys

Problem solving techniques are valuable at home and at work. I have used these processes informally with both Teagan and Jimmy to overcome both school problems and issues encountered at home. During a Marriage Team course, Sheri and I used a more formal problem solving process to resolve a priority conflict between a home project and a family visit. As you read the next few sections, keep in mind these tools can be used both formally and informally at home and at work.

Kevin opened the meeting with an intense look in his eyes. "We've become complacent. It seems we spend too much time discussing all that is well rather than pinpointing where we are deficient. Don't get me wrong; I enjoy and understand the need to celebrate our successes, but not at the risk of resting on our laurels. We are only as strong as our weakest link, and in order to maintain an advantage, we need to improve in the right areas. We need to learn and practice exception management." Raj looked confused, so Kevin offered the following quote by John Templeton regarding contrarian investment:

Today, as in the time of the South Sea Bubble, human nature is drawn like a moth to the flame by the speculative fads of the marketplace. The excitement of new glamour issues in electronics or medical technology, the general euphoria over a rising market; these lure even many experienced investors. Their optimism overcomes their better judgment. They abandon critical analysis of the investment's fundamental value. Like gamblers in a casino they play against the odds, paying inflated prices and dreaming of quick profit.

A contemporary social psychologist uses the term "groupthink" to describe the modern manifestation of crowd madness. Groupthink represents the prevailing beliefs and rationalization that all too often influence the decision even of experts. Their investment advice is shaped by the opinions of others, not by the rigors of their own independent analysis.

It takes patience, discipline and courage to follow the "contrarian" route to investment success: to buy when others are despondently selling, to sell when others are avidly buying…However, based on half a century of experience, I can attest to the rewards at the end of the journey. The best way for an investor to avoid popular delusions is to focus not on outlook, but on value.

Kevin continued, "It takes patience, discipline, courage, and consideration to be a contrarian manager. We need to empower teams and learn to focus our attention on topics that bring the most future value. We need a process to identify risks and problems before they manifest, to prevent taking a hit under the waterline. Such a process will be far more valuable than pondering our past and current successes. We cannot steer by our wake. I do not suggest that we turn into a bunch of crepehangers [pessimistic worriers] running around wearing black hats and ridiculing one another—only that we don't become stuck in a rut of optimistic groupthink, burying core issues. We need to be pragmatically optimistic, alert to upsides while diligently breaking down barriers. Key performance indicators, customer surveys, new product reviews, and even goal reviews should highlight deficiencies rather than emphasize past success. Yesterday's business processes may be sufficient today and perhaps adequate tomorrow but likely insufficient next year and dilapidated in five. Rather than letting our processes fall behind for several years, we need to proactively engage at all levels in a process of continuous improvement."

Raj was pumped: "Let's get started!" Kevin requested that they reconvene the next day with the addition of Jim, his friend and CEO of a productivity-software company. Raj agreed; he too knew Jim and thought his expertise would be useful.

They dove in bright and early the next morning. Kevin reviewed his objectives to get everyone on the same page.

- Focus attention on projects that promise to generate value now and in the future.
- Celebrate successes, but relentlessly track down and allay risks and problems.
- Face the fact that we need to improve more rapidly than our competitors; put the company on a path of continuous improvement.

Jim listened intently. Kevin finished by sharing his thoughts pertaining to contrarian and exception management. The room grew momentarily silent as they pondered the day ahead. Jim broke the silence: "Let's attempt to avoid becoming bogged down with deep philosophical discussions and intricate definitions. Do you each agree that what we need here is 'good enough for now' and scalable for the future, reserving the majority of development resources for products and services?" Nods and grunts of approval followed. "Let's define support processes that are good enough for today, sufficient for tomorrow, and capable of improvement as needed to address your dynamic market." Kevin and Raj again nodded in agreement.

Jim continued, "Many define an efficient manager as one who quickly assimilates volumes of data and input from multiple sources. He or she filters, sorts, and sifts, and without hesitation or doubt, makes decisions, divvies out assignments, and moves on. Sound about right?"

Again, nods of agreement. "We will define a contrarian manager as one who hires capable employees, invests in training as necessary, ensures that the information flows first to those in his or her organization who need the data to make decisions, and empowers his team to decide according to a predetermined level of empowerment. This manager is keenly aware of *when* key decisions are required, and if there are no advantages to early decisions, is content to wait in hopes that—" At this point, Jim paused and then counted off each following point on his fingers for emphasis: "(1) By waiting until necessary, more data will become available, enabling a better decision; (2) our team of experts, armed with better data, will arrive at a decision prior to the drop-dead date, obviating the need for management to decide; (3) together we are smarter than any one of us; and (4) the team will better appreciate management involvement if they are stifled and cannot arrive at a decision on their own."

Kevin thought about this. "So you're saying we should hire experts, let them do their jobs, and only intercede when necessary?"

"Basically, yes. The trick is knowing *when*—and having processes that indicate when a hands-off approach is okay and when a hands-on approach is necessary."

Jim provided a quick overview of the see-plan-do-get process, team dynamics, management by objectives, and SMART goals, emphasizing that the process needs to connect long-term vision to short-term actions and deliverables. He concluded, "Your process needs to be pervasive—not confined to some silos or excluded from others. Adopt one process and improve it as a team. Differentiate your products and services from those provided by your competitors. Use standardization of process within your walls to drive differentiation outside your walls."

It did not take long to agree on a process that would link the company's vision to high-level goals, high-level goals to more refined departmental and individual goals, and those to even more detailed tasks (Figure 17), and with that, develop a process to facilitate problem identification. Jim cautioned the team that many managers conduct meetings with their teams in order to review progress, hoping to leave feeling good about everything—often endeavoring to avoid conflict rather than facing problems and removing barriers (which should be the primary focus of status meetings). Kevin and Raj excitedly agreed to use the system and process that Jim and his company had developed.

Jim's team introduced their process, which employs one system to capture company visions and team missions, establish and track goals, link goals to projects, monitor tasks associated with projects or daily to-do lists, and to categorize status of each goal, deliverable, or task using a common set of indicators:

- **Complete:** Met or exceeded schedule, cost, and performance targets
- **Partial:** Completed task late, but delivered all cost and performance requirements or was close enough to meeting some or all of the targets that key stakeholders agreed the intent of the task was partially achieved
- **Missed (closed)**: Closed the task and missed cost, performance, and/or schedule requirements
- **Missed (open)**: Missed schedule but still working to achieve cost and performance requirements
- **Will miss**: Predicted to miss schedule, cost, and/or performance requirements. Recovery or backup plan may be drafted.
- **At risk**: Possibility of missing cost, schedule, and/or performance requirements
- **Requires help/input**: Team has been waiting on information, material, or services that are necessary to proceed and requires help to facilitate delivery.
- **On target**: Proceeding according to plan. Key performance indicators (metrics) are on target with expectations.
- **Not started**: Action planned and pending but not yet started. Ensure the intended start date has not passed.

- **On hold**: No work is ongoing, but project or task may be revisited at some time in the future.
- **Canceled**: Work was not started or has ceased with no expectation of reviving the goal, task, or project at a later date.

The team agreed to conduct problem-solving meetings directly from the system rather than requiring owners to create presentations. They would utilize the team pages from the Cloud Effective productivity app to manage team meetings. The team pages include top-level missions, clearly stated goals, projects, and action boards as well as communication boards to facilitate interaction pertinent to important items rather than items already completed, on hold, or canceled.

During these meetings, recently closed (inactive) items would quickly be reviewed. If root causes of misses are not understood, investigations of tasks with a status of missed (closed) or partial will be scheduled. Review meetings are designed to focus would be on active (Not started-but planned, On Target, Requires input or Help, At Risk, Missed (Open)) rather than dwelling on items that are no longer consuming resources (Complete, Partial, Missed, On Hold, and Canceled). Further, the team agreed that, though they may quickly probe 'On Target' items, they would investigate items tagged as 'Missed (Open),' 'At Risk,' and 'Requires Input/Help.' (Figure 21). Most of the meeting will be spent to reviewing risk-mitigation plans for all deliverables and tasks with the status of will miss, at risk, or missed (open).

Jim, Kevin, and Raj agreed that the risk-mitigation worksheet (Figure 22) is to be used to identify the task owner, team members, task title, and status as reported on the exception page. Additionally, the worksheet includes a trend status indicating whether the situation is improving, stable, or getting worse. There is a description of the desired results and a problem statement outlining the facts and conditions impeding progress, including the potential impact of the not delivering the desired results—why it is an issue and to whom it is

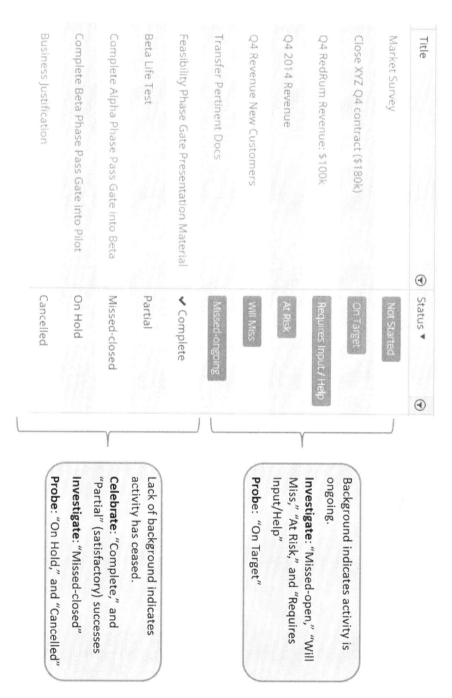

Figure 21: Exception-management table used to quickly identify the status of deliverables and tasks. Screenshot courtesy of Cloud Effective (http://www.CloudEffective.com).

important. Included next is the working hypothesis of the root cause derived by using the five whys, eight steps of problem solving, or a similar process. The five-whys technique is based on the hypothesis that one can arrive at the root cause of a problem by asking "why did that happen?" an average of five times. Some problems may require more or fewer whys. Consider the following example:

1. The room is dark. Why? The light is not on.
2. Why is the light not on? The light is not on because no current is flowing through the light bulb.
3. Why is there no current flowing? Investigate:
   a. Is the switch in the off position? No, the switch is in the on position.
   b. Is the filament broken? No, the bulb is good.
   c. Is the switch broken? No, it appears the switch opens and closes the circuit as designed.
   d. Is there voltage at the switch? No. Current did not flow because there is no live wire at the switch.
4. Why is there no voltage at the switch? Investigate:
   a. Is the circuit breaker tripped? No, the circuit breaker is set.
   b. Is there a GFCI on the circuit? Yes.
   c. Is the GFCI tripped? Yes.
5. Why is the GFCI tripped? Investigate:
   a. Found a hair dryer plugged in and lying in a puddle of water on the counter.
   b. Unplugged the hair dryer, dried the counter, and reset the GFCI. The GFCI did not trip.
   c. Tried the light switch, and the light turned on.

Conclusion: The light was off due to a wet hair dryer that shorted and blew a GFCI receptacle on the same circuit as the light switch.

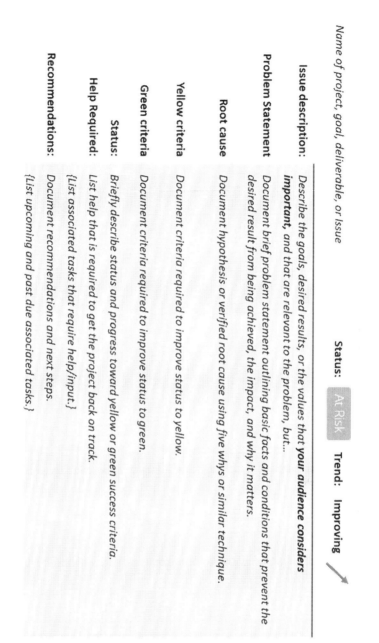

Name of project, goal, deliverable, or issue **Status:** At Risk **Trend:** Improving

Issue description:	*Describe the goals, desired results, or the values that **your audience considers important**, and that are relevant to the problem, but...*
Problem Statement	*Document brief problem statement outlining basic facts and conditions that prevent the desired result from being achieved, the impact, and why it matters.*
Root cause	*Document hypothesis or verified root cause using five whys or similar technique.*
Yellow criteria	*Document criteria required to improve status to yellow.*
Green criteria	*Document criteria required to improve status to green.*
Status:	*Briefly describe status and progress toward yellow or green success criteria.*
Help Required:	*List help that is required to get the project back on track.*
	{List associated tasks that require help/input.}
Recommendations:	*Document recommendations and next steps.*
	{List upcoming and past due associated tasks.}

Figure 22: Risk-mitigation worksheet

Jim and Kevin then recommended that each risk mitigation team identify success criteria (yield, throughput, cycle time, or similar performance measurements) required to move the status from red to yellow and from yellow to green and that the teams should document current status relative to the identified targets. For example, a team may establish that the criteria for moving a product-development project from red to yellow includes achieving a test yield of over 90 percent; and with a yield that is presently only 85 percent, the status is still red, but if the yield was previously only 80 percent, the team can show a trend that is improving. The status statement may read, "This week we achieved a test yield of 85 percent against our target of over 90 percent to move to yellow and over 98 percent to move to green. Our trend is improving. The main yield detractor is power output, and as a result of recent efficiency improvements, the power distribution has shifted, and thus, the yield has improved."

The team may or may not require additional resources, but if resources are required, each request should be accompanied by a list of planned actions with a detailed description of the specific help (action or desired results) that is prescribed. Finally, the team should summarize recommendations and list upcoming actions.

Jim commented that the summary sheet is an excellent tool for management review, but if a problem at hand is particularly difficult, it is likely that a much more rigorous process is required to resolve the problem. He briefly explained the six-sigma DMAIC process as developed by Motorola and the 8D (eight disciplines of problem solving often attributed to the automotive industry) process:

DMAIC:

1. Define the opportunity.
2. Measure current performance.
3. Analyze the current process.
4. Improve process effectiveness (performance, cost, time).
5. Control and adjust new processes.

8D:

1. Prepare and plan.
2. Form a team.
3. Describe the issue. Refine the plan.
4. Contain the problem.

5. Develop a solution (engineering).
6. Validate the solution (production).
7. Implement preventative measures.
8. Celebrate.

Rather than get bogged down in the nuances of how the processes were similar or different, Kevin and Raj agreed to focus on their purpose and implement a process that was likely to be easily understood and adopted. Jim commented, "One of the key differences between 8D and DMAIC is the containment process, and if you analyze the steps required to develop short-term containment for a problem, you will find them to be strikingly similar to the steps required to develop a long-term solution." He paused to compare short- and long-term improvement cycles (Figure 23 and 25 respectively). Jim continued, "The first question that must be asked and answered is 'do you have a problem that is escaping your company or escaping from part of your organization to another?' If the answer is yes, then a quick containment loop is required.

"Form your team. Collect facts and feelings to determine where the likely escape paths exist. Determine how those paths can be contained, which may require halting production of a certain product for a period of time or implementing a rigorous screening process, depending on both the feasibility of developing reliable screening and whether it is more financially prudent to screen or halt. Screening may cost you more money, but stopping may cost more goodwill with your customers. Next, develop and test your containment. If the screen proves to be satisfactory in an engineering environment, move the containment to your production line. Determine if the problem could be affecting other products or other steps in your process; if yes, implement similar containment measures to prevent recurrence elsewhere. Monitor results for all potential escape paths. Determine what you have learned. Continue around the containment loop until the problem is contained. Once contained, move to the long-term improvement loop."

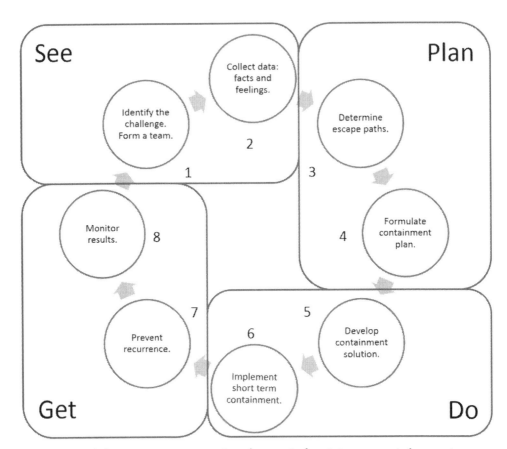

Figure 23: Eight-step process to implement short-term containment

Raj was excited. He liked the consistency and the "obviousness" of the similarities between the short- and long-term solutions. He chimed in, "So the most salient difference between these improvement cycles is the identification and elimination of the root cause. It seems to me that we often stopped after the containment loop, which felt like we were putting a Band-Aid on a seeping wound. I like the thought of executing two loops—the first to mitigate the risk as quickly as possible and then the second to identify and reasonably mitigate the root cause."

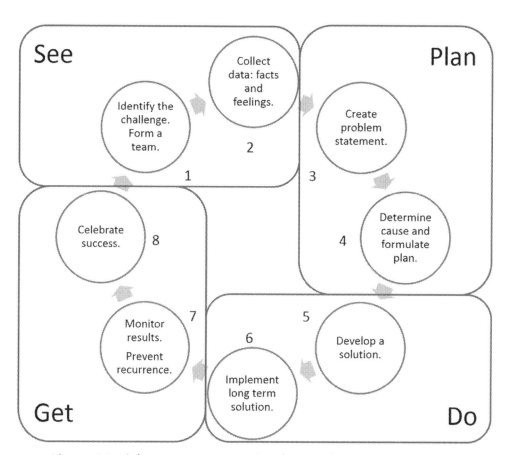

Figure 24: Eight-step process to implement long-term improvement

Jim agreed. "This is a powerful process. Once you have determined and contained escape paths, your team is better positioned to self-evaluate: do they have the correct team members to identify root causes and implement a long-term solution? If not, they need to "reform" the team, adding members with the necessary skill sets. What did they learn during the containment process? What knowledge and data do the new team members bring? What is the desired future state? How does today's reality compare with the desired future state? What is the impact of the issue? Who is affected? Upon addressing these questions, your team should be well positioned to create a clear and concise problem statement. A well-stated problem focuses your team and is a major step in problem resolution (some say a problem clearly stated is half-solved)." Jim went on to explain how to formulate such a statement.

Concisely state how the world would look if the problem did not exist (define the desired future state):

- Describe how you will know if the team is successful.
- What are the metrics of success?
- What are the targets for these metrics? For example, cascaded (rolled) throughput yield is greater than 90 percent.

Clarify the nature of the problem:

- Define a single problem.
- Identify where the problem is appearing.
- Identify where the problem occurs and perhaps where it does not occur.
- Quantify the size of the problem (percentages and numbers). How often and to what extent does the problem occur? Is the problem time dependent, unit dependent, seasonally dependent, and so forth?

Describe the impact:

- How does it affect customers and your organization?
- Whom does it affect? Whom does it not affect?
- What is the cost internally and externally?
- Is there time lost?
- Are there opportunities lost or at risk?

Jim cautioned, "The problem statement is not used to assign blame, guess at a cause, or offer a solution. The problem statement captures the desired future state, clearly describes the gaps between reality and that desired state, and identifies the impact of leaving the problem (gaps) unresolved."

He continued, "Next, develop one or more hypotheses and use the five whys and other investigative techniques, such as fish-bone diagrams, to identify the root cause. When the root cause is identified, the team will generate an engineering solution, and when confident the problem has been resolved in an engineering environment, the team will validate the new processes in production." Jim remarked that the prevention steps were similar to those taken during the short-term containment process but noted a key difference: "Once the long-term solution has been implemented in both the affected process and others that may have eventually been affected, the team should be recognized for its accomplishment. Success should be celebrated." Kevin felt they had made great progress and committed to allocating ample resources to train the team and roll out the new system.

New Product or Process Introduction

Whether at home or at work, creativity is exciting. Individuals and organizations are invigorated when they imagine a "great" new idea. Energy rises. Pulses quicken. Minds are unleashed to seek solutions that once seemed impossible. Why? How does this happen? Similar to recipes followed by chefs or process steps followed by lab technicians, our subconscious minds follow processes to arrive at ideas and decisions (refer to the "Framework of Thought Parts II and III" in *VerAegis—Relationships*). It follows that whether we are skilled chefs, woodworkers, artists, engineers, or scientists, we each benefit when we opt to consciously follow a creativity change management process which mimics our natural subconscious process (Figure 25).

The basic flow (not surprisingly) follows the See-Plan-Do-Get change control process. How we see the world influences our ideas. When we get excited enough about an idea, we search for any and all data we can find to determine plausibility, and if still excited, we intuitively define our approach, execute, then release and evaluate results before repeating the cycle with our next idea. Consider a professional artist who has just come up with an idea for their next painting in a series of paintings depicting the struggle of humankind's coexistence with nature. The artist sees the image in her mind. She determines that this painting will depict humankind's drive to "develop" our planet in direct conflict with our need to protect natural resources. The artist can visualize the image and optimistically contemplates this important message and the different mediums available. She considers her skill set and begins to plan her approach. She tests her idea first with a few

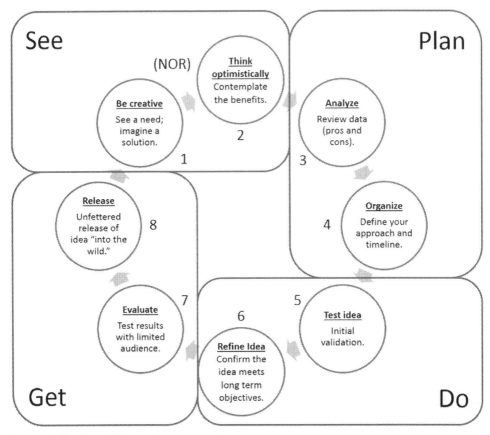

Figure 25: Creativity change control process

rough sketches, then moves to a large canvas. Once a canvas sketch meets her satisfaction, she proceeds to an underpainting. Now confident her idea will deliver the intended impact, she begins to refine the idea, meticulously building layer upon layer. She shows the painting to a few colleagues, her agent, and her husband. Armed with constructive feedback, she adds the final touches and hangs the work in her gallery for all to see while her team begins the duplication process for a five-hundred-unit limited release. This artist has followed a process. Perhaps written, perhaps not, but it is a process nevertheless.

Why follow such a process to develop new concepts? Will a defined process not stifle the creative cycle required to innovate? Will it not impede creative genius? Don't great ideas occur more like lightning strikes than a deliberate process? In reality, some ideas are spontaneous, but most are the result of considerable preparation, deliberate brainstorming, and concentrated effort. We each will follow a process; whether the process is repeatable and predictable is a choice. However, when making that choice, we must face the reality that most individuals and companies cannot rely on random events to propel them into the future and ensure a competitive edge. As the pace of technological advances accelerates, innovation's importance to the individuals and companies of the world has never been greater. Should the process be deliberate or left to chance? The stark reality is that winning ideas are rarer than most believe and so cannot be left to chance. "For every one thousand ideas, only one hundred will have enough commercial promise to merit a small-scale experiment, only ten of those will warrant a substantial financial commitment, and of those, only a couple will turn out to be unqualified successes." (Gary Hamel)

Creativity and innovation are processes. Left to chance, the odds of repeated success are low, whereas a disciplined, repeatable approach will increase predictability and decrease variation, cost of development, and time to market. "An elite 30 percent of firms do achieve an enviable 80 percent success rate; that is, 80 percent of the resources they spend on innovation goes to new product winners. These few firms show that it is possible to outperform the average, and by a considerable margin, if you use a systematic process" (Innovation 2001).

These elite firms achieve success by executing a systematic process to manage all stages of new product or process innovation (NPI). Creativity is the ability of a person or team to escape the confines of traditional ideas, rules, or patterns to generate new

ideas, designs, or products that until imagined were completely nonexistent. To be successful, engineers, scientists, researchers, artists, writers, lawyers, individuals, and teams must learn to manage this creative process from the moment of ideation to the moment of fruition.

To be a successful change leader, an enterprise has to have a policy of systematic innovation. Innovation is not a "flash of genius." It is hard work. And this work should be organized as a regular part of every unit within the enterprise, and of every level of management.

Peter Drucker

Before diving deeply into an innovation process, it is prudent to define our individual goals or the needs of our business. The ultimate success of any innovation process will be measured by its ability to meet higher-level objectives and visions. To sustain success, individuals, small businesses, and larger companies need to create value and, in turn, profits; even nonprofit organizations need to generate ample cash to cover expenses and enable future investment. Consequently, we need to have a strategy that enables us to generate profits now and in the future, which in turn requires that we provide value to the market (customers, shareholders, community, etc.). Finally, in order to ensure longevity, we also need to provide a secure and satisfying environment for employees, colleagues and others we rely on to accomplish our goals. We must remain respectfully candid (openly and respectfully raising issues even when doing so is uncomfortable), engage in a path of continuous improvement, embrace a culture of self-discipline and entrepreneurial spirit, empower people to make decisions, and communicate clearly and decisively both what we choose to do and what we choose to not do.

A steady stream of new and successful products and services delivered to the market, as well as continuously improved operational efficiencies, is essential to achieving these three high-level visions (generating profits, providing value, and creating a positive work environment). In other words, we must achieve and maintain a competitive advantage through a combination of technical differentiation (strategic positioning) and operational effectiveness. Strategic positioning is providing unique, superior products or services that offer more value to customers than rivals' comparable products or services. Operational effectiveness is performing similar activities (operational competencies) better than rivals perform them—for example, adhering to an NPI process that ensures 80 percent of development resources are deployed on winning products. Therefore, a competitive advantage is defined as outperforming rivals, now and in the future, by establishing a sustainable difference via a combination of operational and strategic competencies.

One of the more difficult challenges of NPI is the ability to hit a specific, often fleeting market window. Successful innovation requires velocity. Velocity represents more than speed alone—more than time to market. Velocity represents speed *and* direction. Many great ideas die simply because they are too slow, but others die because they enter the wrong market or never had a market to begin with. The direction chosen is as important as the time required to arrive. High velocity yields a competitive advantage, increases response to customers' needs, and decreases the time to market. Often, the first-to-market product wins, even over a product that is better but later. Early in my career, I was developing a new higher-power semiconductor laser. My launch customer needed to begin qualification in January. I delivered parts in March. He loved the lasers; they were better than our competitors'—higher powered and more efficient. But it didn't matter. He and his team were already two months into a qualification process. We had missed our window.

Fortunately, there were several more customers who purchased our design, and we were able to move the product into production, but I never forgot that lesson: good enough and on time often beats better and late. Shorter time to revenue (the time elapsed between commencing development and the first product revenue) and the ability to hit a fixed window of opportunity equates to more revenue for a given product's life cycle. Earlier market entry enables next-generation development to begin sooner, increasing the cycles of learning (shorter time means more learning cycles over a given time period). Velocity means fewer surprises: decreased time between concept and commercialization reduces odds that market conditions will change dramatically during development, and when market conditions remain relatively consistent during development, it is less likely that product requirements will change prior to release. Finally, being first to market establishes a leadership position, increases customer confidence, and establishes customer loyalty.

Many argue that following an NPI process slows innovation by constraining teams. This may be true for ill-conceived processes, but well-thought-out NPI processes deliver better results sooner with increased probability of success. Dr. Norm Kuchar of General Electric found that formalized development techniques were responsible for a decrease in time to market of greater than 25 percent. Kevin's team bought in to the concept. They had been burned by cutting corners, finding it necessary to "return to the drawing board" once products failed in the customers' hands. They had also missed market windows. Sure, they had enjoyed successes, but they felt they could do better. Raj, Theresa, Toni, and Tom each reviewed what they had learned about NPI. They searched files, notes, and memories to recall successes and failures as well as accelerators and detractors of their recent product-development projects. Once armed with data, they compiled the objectives they agreed were required of a successful NPI process.

First and foremost, adherence to the process must ensure 80 percent or more of their product- and process-development resources are allocated to winning products. Proper allocation of resources to winners demands two things: (1) proper assessment of new opportunities to quickly and accurately disposition both incremental and potentially disruptive opportunities; and (2) a decisive process to cull losing opportunities as early as possible.

The NPI process must also ensure that the appropriate level of resources is allocated based on the complexity of the new product or process development effort. All new products and processes are subject to the NPI process—no exceptions. The NPI process is not a fad or a temporary fix to motivate the troops; it is a way of life for companies striving for sustained success and thus must be flexible enough to address relatively simple and considerably complex efforts.

A successful NPI process also requires quick and effective responses to market demands and customer inquiries. The team must set a reasonable first-response time goal of twenty-four to forty-eight hours for all new opportunity inquiries, providing either a quote, a no bid, or a target date for which a quote will be available in the case of products that require development (they are subject to the NPI phase-gate development process).

Realizing that most of their problems with customers stemmed from missed expectations, they agreed that through the new process, sales and marketing should align customer expectations based on the state of the product relative to the phase-gate process. Finally, and perhaps most importantly, they agreed that the new process needed to be intimately integrated with the MBO process. Only then could they ensure that NPI projects and subsequent resource allocation were free from conflict with other key objectives.

Based on experience and literature review, the team defined the steps required to move a product through its cradle-to-grave life cycle: (1) discovery and initial planning; (2) feasibility (prototype and breadboard development) and refined planning; (3) development (alpha); (4) reliability and reproducibility (beta); (5) limited release (pilot); (6) full release (production); and (7) end of life (EOL).

Recall the new-opportunity review (NOR) developed by Toni and Tom. New opportunities will stem from new capabilities, new markets, or incremental enhancements in existing markets, leading to the introduction of new products and the demise of older ones. Jim pointed out that though new product innovation occurs mainly in the discovery to initial-release phases, the life cycle process requires a feedback loop from the end of life to a new beginning in order to improve the NPI process. Thus, for certain purposes, the product life cycle is better illustrated as a see-plan-do-get change management loop rather than a linear series of events (Figure 26).

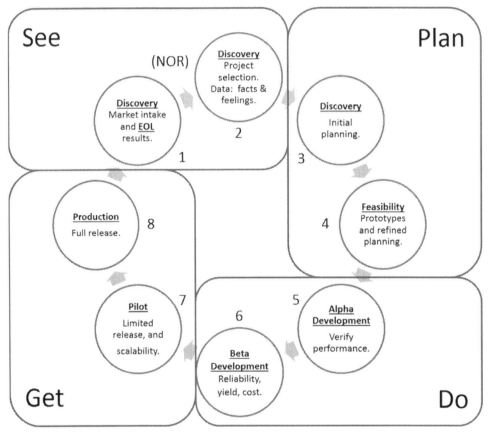

Figure 26: Product or process life-cycle management loop

How you and your team see the world, your marketplace, your customers, and opportunities—your paradigm—is shaped by past successes and failures, market trends, and customer inquiries. Similarly, the new-opportunity review is shaped by the way you and your team view the world. The NOR and project-selection processes are meant to occur during the earliest stages of discovery and are designed to be simple, expedient, and effective tools to cull losers, capitalize on no-brainers, and launch all other ideas deeper into the initial planning phase of the product life cycle. The basic purpose of the phase-gate process is to screen losers prior to spending too much money. Early elimination of losers is the only way to possibly allocate 80 percent of development spending to winners (Figure 27). This process, moving an idea from discovery through fruition, is useful whether running a company or a household, though the rigor and details of execution will vary greatly. In other words, these NPI phases and concepts are applicable whether one is developing space shuttles, lasers, cupcakes, science-fair projects, a remodeled kitchen, or anything in between—though the details necessary to achieve success vary proportionally to scale and complexity, and whether the project is a 'one-off' or a product destined for mass distribution.

Discovery

The main purpose of discovery is to develop a clear understanding of the market opportunity and formulate a business case, a product concept, and a preliminary product specification. In many companies, most of the effort during discovery is handled by sales and marketing and product-line management (PLM), with truly few development and finance resources required. Many ideas may not make it past a lunch meeting or dinner with a client, but those that do will require more preparation prior to being presented as new opportunities. In the same vane, your significant other may harbor many dreams, lend an ear, but take heart, not all dreams merit detailed consideration or even any critical thinking. Let the dreamer dream. Attempt to understand and perhaps optimistically contribute to the upside, but be prepared with this phased process should the dreamer decide to embark upon the journey so that you are in position to contribute to

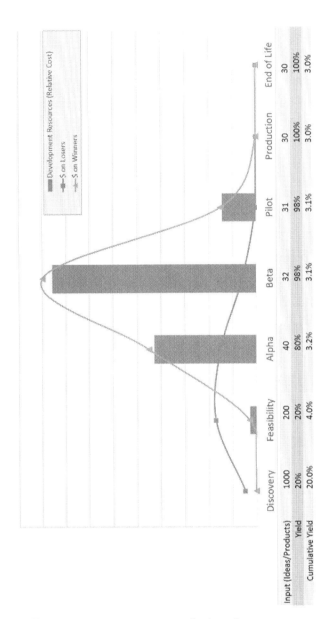

Input (Ideas/Products)	Discovery	Feasibility	Alpha	Beta	Pilot	Production	End of Life
	1000	200	40	32	31	30	30
Yield	20%	20%	80%	98%	98%	100%	100%
Cumulative Yield	20.0%	4.0%	3.2%	3.1%	3.1%	3.0%	3.0%

Figure 27: Allocating 80 percent of development resources to winning products means culling losers early, while development costs are low.

success and limit exposure. Develop and review more-detailed descriptions of the opportunity, product positioning, and value statements as well as market and product requirements. I've provided the following prompts in order to facilitate this process.

Define the Opportunity

Use the following as an example to create an opportunity definition:

The [conceptual product] is a [product or service type] that addresses the top requirements in the [identify the specific market or markets] by specifically addressing [note the applications, services, accessibility improvements, and so on]. These requirements are (1) satisfying emerging market requirements: [list key emerging market requirements] and/or established market requirements: [note established market requirements] of the [list the specific market or markets], (2) increasing customer satisfaction via improved [list user experiences and product performance improvements], and (3) entering the market by [specific time frame] in order to be first to serve the XYZ market.

Set clear priorities as follows:

[Choose one of the main attributes—cost, schedule, or performance] is the top priority. The must-have product requirements for launch are [list key performance indicators and cost criteria]. Performance attributes of secondary importance will be relaxed if they threaten to increase cost or delay release.

Summarize Positioning, Value Proposition, and Market

Similarly, a concise positioning statement can be written as follows:

For [target market/end user], who wants or needs [compelling reason to buy]. The [product name] is a [product category] that provides [key benefits]. Unlike [main competitor(s)], the [product name] has [key differentiation linked to the compelling reason to buy].

The target market, market size, and primary customer base for product [product name] is [target market, total market size in revenue, top customer segments], respectively. We expect to win [X percent] market share by [expected time frame].

Define both the performance and schedule requirements for success. List key performance metrics. Distinguish between the must-haves and the nice-to-haves. Must-haves are core performance metrics that, if absent, lead to certain failure. For example, you cannot provide cupcakes that don't taste good, and you cannot sell cars that are not equipped with wheels and tires. Nice-to-haves are options and features that, if absent, may not distinguish you from the competition but will not prevent reasonable success. Nice-to-haves will enhance your product or service when combined with must-haves, but alone will not enable access to desired markets. It is also important during the discovery phase to define pricing, cost, and volume targets. Price is the amount of money customers will pay for your product or service, whereas cost is the amount of money required from you or your company to provide the product or service. Volume is a forecast of the number of units or service hours to be sold over a specific time period.

Most often, your product or service will have competition, and timing is a key element to winning customers and market share, but schedule should not come at the expense of managing projects properly. Cutting corners to save time does not pay. Do it right the first time; there is seldom time to do it over. Effective MBO and SMART goal processes used in conjunction with an NPI process better position your team for cross-functional success.

Whether working solo or with others, discovery is meant to be an early stage ideation phase allowing for less costly screening of losers (Figure 27). As a rule of thumb, 80 percent of ideas created during discovery should be culled, whereas only 20 percent, or two hundred of every thousand ideas, should pass. Few development resources are required during discovery. The majority of new ideas will be rejected by an individual or a combination of sales, marketing, and product-line managers (those responsible for the cradle-to-grave life cycle of products) who decide no further effort is merited.

During discovery, evaluate how the product concept fits with your overall mission and strategy. Define your competitive advantage and the compelling reason your customers will buy from you. Ensure that the business potential warrants further investment, and finally, ensure that the necessary resources are available for deployment (especially those required for the next phase). Develop a checklist of items required in either preliminary or comprehensive form in order to exit the discovery phase and enter the feasibility phase. Examples include a favorable financial analysis, clearly articulated resource requirements, a general overall program plan and a comprehensive feasibility plan.

The Planning and Feasibility Phase

The intent of the planning and feasibility phase is to inexpensively, quickly, and decisively determine which ideas are feasible and which are not. The rule of thumb for this phase is to screen 80 percent of the ideas that passed the gate to exit discovery and enter feasibility. In other words, cull another 160 ideas, passing only about 4 percent of the total input funnel, or 40 of the original 1,000 ideas, into full development (alpha). Emphasize low-cost methods, such as quick sketches, draft concepts, computer simulation and "benchtop" experiments, to determine feasibility. Avoid heavy investment in material and equipment until initial experiments and a refined business case indicate that further investment is advisable.

Complete a comprehensive analysis of product requirements (must-haves and nice-to-haves) as well as initial and growth markets. Identify early adopters (those customers who are willing to take risks on early-release products in order to take advantage of the latest and greatest improvements) and develop your marketing and distribution plan to reach a broader customer base. In order to enter full development, the business case must be favorable and feasibility demonstrated; in other words, there must be better-than-reasonable expectations that the product or service will meet customer requirements and be profitable. Resources must be available for allocation, team members identified, SMART goals in place, project plans established, and your competitive advantage refined. You must know how (and where) you will gain advantage over your closest competition and what barriers exist that prevent competitors from quickly duplicating your product or approach.

The Alpha Development Phase

The main objective of the alpha development phase is to design a salable product or service that meets broad market (when applicable) and key customer requirements (cost, schedule, and performance). Development spending is highest during the alpha and beta development phases, so it is important that the heavy culling is completed prior to entering alpha. Recall that 96 percent of the original ideas have now been screened, or, in other words, only forty of one thousand have been passed into alpha and merit full scale investment (time and materials).

Aim to screen 20 percent or less during alpha development, passing 80 percent, or 32, into beta. Establish initial development trials to probe your must-haves and determine early on if the product should be culled in order to prevent spending too much on a loser (Figure 27: Allocating 80 percent of development resources to winning products means culling losers early, while development costs are low. The early trials during alpha are aimed at achieving targeted form, fit, and function, as opposed to less costly computer and benchtop tests performed in feasibility. When cost is higher, haphazard trial-and-error approaches should be avoided. However, experiments that test one factor at a time do serve a purpose, especially when trying to determine physical limits. Once limits are understood, use design of experiment (DOE) techniques (multivariable experimental techniques first developed in the 1920s to optimize agricultural yields) to more quickly hone in on your desired results. Start with screening DOEs to identify your most important variables (e.g., Taguchi) and then progress to modeling designs (e.g., full factorial or central composite) in order to leverage the power of statistics to increase both your physical and intuitive understanding. Dr. Norm Kuchar, who, under Jack Welch, was responsible for the worldwide deployment of General

Electric's design for six sigma (DFSS) program, found that DOE and other DFSS techniques were responsible for a decrease in time to market of greater than 25 percent, developmental cost reduction of 20 to 40 percent, and an increase in product quality (30 to 35 percent narrower distributions) at the time of launch.

Customer feedback is another crucial element of development. I have encountered many development engineers who resist early engagement with customers for fear that the product is "not ready." Without customer feedback, however, it is more difficult to ensure you are on the correct path. Does your product work correctly? Is it easy and intuitive to use? Does it fit? Is it easy to handle? If it is a food, does it taste good? Make no mistake—it is imperative to engage with early adopters and obtain critical feedback once the product promises to meet the agreed upon key performance indicators. But these engagements should be orchestrated. The product should be marked as alpha, and expectations should be set accordingly—for example, "The product is in the early development stages, and we are soliciting performance feedback to determine if the design is satisfactory."

Cost, pricing, and business models should be updated during the alpha phase based on customer feedback, design reviews, and product performance. An agreed-upon design, favorable internal and customer feedback, and sound financial models (showing profitability with believable cost, pricing, and volume forecasts) are required to exit alpha and enter beta development.

The Beta Development Phase

The beta phase is the final development phase in the product life cycle. The main objective of the beta development phase is to establish that the product meets market needs and that customer feedback continues to be favorable. Determine with confidence that the product or service can be delivered by those who will be responsible for doing so in future phases (such as manufacturers, producers, cooks, consultants, etc.), and confirm that they are able to deliver without assistance from development resources and to repeatedly meet performance and reliability requirements within expected cost targets. In other words, demonstrate that the product or service is repeatable, reliable, and affordable. Continued customer feedback is vital to ensuring the repeatability and usability of the design.

Development spending continues to be high during performance reliability and repeatability tests, as the volume and costs of tests are increasing. Recall that nearly 97 percent of the original ideas have been screened, or, in other words, only thirty-two of one thousand have survived early phases to reach the beta phase. The sunk costs of the thirty-two are much higher now, so as a rule of thumb, in order to achieve 80 percent allocation of development spending toward winners, 98 percent of products that reach reliability and repeatability testing should pass. Aim to screen 2 percent or less during beta development, passing 98 percent, or thirty-one, into your pilot launch. Note that this requires that earlier culling is sufficient, so that only one of every thirty-two products that reach beta is subsequently rejected (Figure 27: Allocating 80 percent of development resources to winning products means culling losers early, while development costs are low. The early trials during beta are aimed at refining the process required for your ongoing production team to be successful. Once again, costs are higher, so trial-and-error approaches that test one factor at a time should be avoided and statistical methods employed.

Continued customer feedback is crucial to ensuring that products or services delivered by production teams meet or exceed expectations. Without customer feedback, however, it is more difficult to ensure that training has been adequate. Recall that such engagements should be orchestrated. The product should be marked as beta, and expectations should be set accordingly: "We are in the final development stage of [name of product or service] and are soliciting performance feedback to determine if we meet or exceed your expectations."

Cost, pricing, and business models should be updated during the beta phase based on customer feedback, design reviews, and product performance. Agreed-upon design and operational procedures, favorable internal and customer feedback, and sound financial models (showing profitability with believable cost, pricing, and volume forecasts) are required to exit beta and initiate your initial (pilot) launch.

The Pilot Phase

The main objectives of the pilot phase are to (1) test sales and marketing to ensure the expected volume comes to fruition prior to committing to a full ramp of production, and (2) ensure the customer fulfillment operation is running smoothly. Determine with confidence that the market is real and that the intended product or service can be delivered independently to multiple customers at increasing volumes, repeatedly meeting performance and reliability requirements within expected cost targets. Aim to screen 2 percent or less during pilot development, passing 98 percent, or thirty of thirty-one, into full release (production) (Figure 27).

Continued customer feedback is beneficial in ensuring that delivered products or services meet or exceed expectations. Bookings and backlogs should be evaluated against plan. Cost, pricing, and business models should be updated during the pilot phase. The ramp plan (the plan to match increased customer demand with increased production volume) and future investment are dependent on market traction and customer orders, as well as sound financial models (showing profitability with believable cost, pricing, and volume forecasts). Future investment in the product is merited only if adequate profitability is achievable and believable.

The Production Phase

By following a disciplined NPI (Discovery through Beta) process, many successful companies are able to allocate 80% of development resources to winning product—which in turn requires that approximately 75% of products that enter Alpha will make it to production. Note, many products in low volume high mix markets will not require both pilot and production phases. Once in production, certainly few, if any, development resources are required. Internal product "owners" (sometimes referred to as product engineers) should be engaged directly with PLMs, sales, marketing, and operations to ensure the product is a success in the marketplace. At this stage, products and services are subject to continuous improvement ("new and improved") until a future product or service is in development that renders the current one obsolete.

End of Life (EOL) to a New Beginning

In order to initiate timely development of the next generation, an astute product owner determines early on that a product or service is on the verge of obsolescence. Ideally, the next generation ramps up as the current generation ramps down, but a smooth transition does not happen without planning. The objectives of this phase are to manage customer expectations, manage any existing inventory, and, ideally, transition your existing customers the old to a new product. Support customers by continuing to meet their needs during product transitions. Provide notice and set reasonable expectations. Fulfill last-time buys. Manage inventories. Determine if ongoing service will be required for your product, and if so, how it will be provided and for what time period. If possible, transition all customers to the new generation.

Finally, review the entire life cycle of the product. Was it a major or marginal success? Or was it a flop that should have been screened? What lessons have been learned and are available to guide future development projects?

Tracks and Traction

Toni, Theresa, and Tom were wrapping up their presentation of the proposed NPI and Product Life Cycle process to Kevin's entire staff when they noticed a look of consternation on Kevin's face. Jim noticed it too. "Kevin, you look concerned," he said. Kevin was quiet for a moment and then stated, "This process sounds comprehensive, but I am concerned that it will bog us down. Do you believe all products will require this rigorous process?"

Toni and Tom smiled. Toni started, "Kevin, recall the new-opportunity review process we established a few months ago. We agreed to adopt the simple yet powerful project-selection process to facilitate determination of which projects are subject to the NPI process, which do not require new processes or products, and which do not merit further review, which, by the way, is part of the idea culling process. Those that require further evaluation will complete the requirements of the discovery planning phase. Further, we established guidelines to categorize the opportunities into specific 'tracks,' defining which phases of development are required for each new project."

Tom continued, "These tracks are designed to match the rigor of the process to the complexity of the development. We have proposed three NPI tracks, with a fourth devoted to new opportunities that initially seem to require a new product but upon further review are found to be addressable by existing products. In summary, we propose the following." Tom began to present a list of tracks. "Track zero—to address new opportunities with existing, qualified products. No phased development required. Then we have track one to address opportunities that can be realized by deploying a new combination of existing product platforms configured in a new way."

At this point, Tom moved toward the tray of cupcakes located on a side table in the meeting room. Selecting two, he observed, "Suppose these cupcakes represent our products. This chocolate cupcake has chocolate frosting, and this white cupcake has vanilla frosting. Suppose a customer desires a chocolate cupcake with vanilla frosting. We have the chocolate cake recipe, and we have the vanilla frosting recipe; we need only to combine these two existing 'platforms' to ensure they meet our customer's expectations. In other words, once we have determined that the market opportunity is real, we pass discovery and move directly to beta for performance validation—no feasibility or product development required beyond the due diligence of discovery and the validation of performance in beta!"

Tom continued, "Then we have track two to address opportunities that can be realized by modifying one or more existing platforms. Consider again the cupcake analogy. Suppose we continually receive requests for strawberry cupcakes with strawberry, vanilla, or chocolate frosting. We have vanilla and chocolate frosting already, but we need to develop both the strawberry cake and frosting. Our bakery chef (the development team) believes we can start from existing 'platforms' (the white cake and vanilla frosting recipes) to develop the strawberry-flavored cake and frosting. Thus, we simply need to modify the recipes for a fairly quick development cycle, moving expeditiously to beta product testing.

"And then, finally, we have track three to address opportunities that require entirely new platforms. And though we will choose products that are a strategic fit and leverage our core competencies, some may require new processes and perhaps new materials and technologies as well. Consider once again our cupcake analogy. Perhaps after encountering a growing clientele interested in gluten-free products, we consider creating a line of gluten-free cupcakes and muffins. Many of our core competencies will be utilized, but the materials (ingredients) and processes will change and require development and testing. In this case, the feasibility will likely consist of market studies, existing recipe options, and the like, but we will require product development and customer trials before the new platform is approved."

Kevin was quiet for a moment. Slowly a smile appeared on his face. "Let me repeat what I believe you have proposed: We will use the voice of the customer and market information to define new opportunities that will address market demands. We will adopt a phased product life-cycle process that consists of seven total and four development phases. Additionally, we will have four tracks to determine which phases are applicable for a given new opportunity: track zero for new opportunities addressed by existing products; track one, the fast track, for quick and easy semicustom designs achieved by combining existing platforms and processes in new ways, which will require discovery and beta; track two for slightly more intricate changes to existing platforms and designs, but still based on existing processes and technologies and requiring the discovery, alpha, and beta phases; and finally, track three, the most rigorous, used to develop new platforms, new processes, and new technologies. Track three will require discovery, feasibility, alpha, and beta phases."

Toni and Tom nodded in agreement. Jim added, "The three-track development process needs to become part of the corporate differentiation strategy. There should be a working checklist that is used to guide teams through each track, and clear kill/go criteria are imperative. Additionally, this phased process approach provides a method to scope projects quickly and effectively, to ensure each aligns with long-term strategies, to ensure innovation resources are assigned to the best-choice winning products, and to identify and pursue opportunities that align with key technical core competencies. Furthermore, we've already reviewed this process with both your custom systems and agile software-development teams. We've addressed their initial concerns, and they are on board. The custom systems development team decided to use the phased NPI process to establish processes, infrastructure, and redeployable subcomponents necessary to develop custom systems in low volume (one to tens of units) and often for single customers. The agile software-development team determined that they could move through the same phases (similar to crawl, walk, run, and then fly), cycling through many agile development steps during each major phase. They will define the performance metrics and must-haves for each phase to enable their software to move to the next level of performance and expectations."

Kevin was clearly pleased. "Thank you," he said. "This is an easy decision. Let's proceed."

Making Good Decisions Is Key to Being Effective

Consistently making good decisions is a prerequisite of leading a balanced and effective life. Throughout your life, you will individually make many conscious and even more subconscious decisions and you will also participate in group decisions. There exist many types of group decisions: unilateral (one person decides for the group), subgroup (a small portion of the team decides for the whole), majority rule (the faction with the greatest number decides for the group), consensus (similar to majority rule, except that all input is considered and likely influences the outcome), and so on. Whether individual or group, all decisions fall into one of two categories: those that need to be made instantly and those that do not. Individuals and groups tend to get into trouble when they mix the two.

Have you ever said anything in the heat of the moment that you wished you could take back? Words hurt. They damage relationships and opportunities. Take a moment to engage your brain prior to engaging your mouth, and use reason whenever time permits. Take time to decide on an appropriate response. Certain situations do require split (emotion-based) decisions: life-and-death combat, fast-paced sports, and most emergency situations. Recall that Dodge (refer to "Framework of Thought, Part III" in *VerAegis—Relationships*) first escaped the firestorm by employing his emotional flight response but ultimately survived by applying reason and creative thinking. Recall also that without emotions, we become paralyzed, unable to make even simple decisions (recall Phineas and Elliott). Just as Plato's charioteer cannot move without his emotional horsepower, neither can we. So, in effect, for many (or most) decisions, we should engage reason and then emotions. Remember to be especially wary of emotions in certain situations, such as gambling, investing, or even shopping; be alert to loss or gain situations that invoke undue feelings of loss aversion (pessimism) or excessive optimism or joy. Marketers are paid to play on our emotions, so we pull that slot lever and make that impulse purchase. In these and similar situations, consult reason first and foremost; crunch the numbers, and then listen to emotions.

We have been "programmed" in our society to admire those who are able to make split decisions. It may appear that Kevin made a split decision to adopt the phase-gate process proposed by Tom, Toni, Theresa, and Jim, but that is not the case. Kevin engaged early on with

Jim and his own staff to set guidelines. Kevin presented a vision, defined a desired end state, and provided metrics of success. The team met several times to review progress, implemented and tested the NOR process, and met with many leaders within the organization to critically analyze the process and then innovatively address the potential pitfalls. Kevin's team was aligned and had already embraced the process. The "split decision" by Kevin was preceded by much analysis, a refined presentation, and several decisions made by trusted and fully capable team members and colleagues. Kevin listened to their presentation. He asked questions, formulated his thoughts, restated the team's position to their satisfaction, listened to his gut, and finally decided that the phased product life-cycle process was a go.

Split decisions are dependent on instinct, intuition, and insight. Instincts are natural abilities or skills. Perhaps you have heard people comment, "His instinct for making the most of each opportunity is amazing." Intuition is similar and often thought of as a sixth sense. It is the ability to understand something without the need for conscious reasoning—you may have heard the expression: "We shall allow our intuition to guide us." Meanwhile, insight is the capacity to gain an accurate and deep understanding of someone or something and is often a combination of instinct and experience. Together, insight, instinct, and intuition are powerful. They are each mechanisms for detecting an unusual blip on the radar; they form the sense that enables a quarterback to quite amazingly move away from *unseen* pressure in the pocket and then find the open receiver. They form the ability of the batter to "know" whether the ball will curve and if he or she should remain in the box to drive the ball into the outfield. Insights are neither taught nor learned; they are instincts honed through diligence and perseverance. It takes devotion to become an expert.

Whenever possible, take your time in making decisions (refer to "Manage Thought" in *VerAegis—Relationships*). The time required is often proportional to the magnitude of the decision. Whether conscious or subconscious, successful decisions require a combination of thinking processes. Thoughts need to be organized. Define and manage the thought process by answering a series of questions: is this decision a personal or team responsibility? Remember that even when the matter is personal, it is good to solicit input from trusted friends and family members. Will the decision be based on familiar and repeating patterns, random events, infrequent events, or a new opportunity that requires an innovative solution? What are the consequences of a good decision? What are the consequences of a bad decision? When does the decision need to be made? What are the downsides of a late decision? Are there benefits to an early decision? When armed with the answers to these questions, an organized approach becomes much more apparent.

Once your thoughts are organized, collect facts and analyze the data. Determine the possible outcomes of your decisions—first the potential benefits, followed by potential obstacles and downsides to each scenario. Remember to review the upsides first; don't mix optimistic and pessimistic thinking. Critical thinking is important, but it has its time. Once upsides are well understood, downsides should then be approached with the intent to resolve them. Use creative thinking and brainstorming techniques to identify solutions to obstacles.

Evaluate the information gathered to date to determine if the proposal "holds water." Evaluate competencies and resources to determine whether the project *can* be done. Evaluate development and product (or service) cost data based on creative thinking, critical thinking, and optimistic thinking sessions and resulting plans and proposals. Evaluate the potential return on investment and alignment to core competencies and strategies to determine whether the project *should* be done. Finally, consult your intuition and feelings: Do you want to do this? Do you feel comfortable or uneasy? If uneasy, is it because of the difficulty, or do you doubt that this is the correct path to pursue? Is the reward not worth the risk? For example, will failure potentially kill your company or deplete your retirement fund, whereas the upside promises only incremental gains?

During a time-sensitive situation that involves evaluation of somewhat predictable and reliable patterns (recall Lieutenant Commander Michael Riley and the Silkworm missile from "Fundamentals of Thought, Part III" in *VerAegis—Relationships*), don't be afraid to "listen to your gut." Interestingly, in situations that align with your natural gifts and in which you have invested the time necessary to become an expert, your subconscious mind quickly follows a nearly identical process to that discussed above for making a conscious decision. Your subconscious first collects and analyzes the data. Then it identifies good omens and upsides. Then it thinks critically to identify bad omens, threats, obstacles, and potential downsides. Finally, the gut feeling kicks in to confirm that everything is fine or to fire dopamine alerts warning of pending threats or great opportunities. In these time-sensitive situations, we need to respond quickly and fluidly to our instincts, but we must be certain that there really is no more time for evaluation and that we are not trying to predict random events.

When faced with random events where past performance cannot be used to predict future performance (gambling, for instance), your subconscious mind follows the same process that it follows for predictable pattern recognition, but it is easily fooled by its aversion to loss or its desire to be rewarded by unexpected outcomes. Recall the Yale students who were outperformed by a rat. Their strong desire to predict a random outcome rendered them less capable than the rodent. In such situations, reason, experience, and analysis are required. If investing in a company, is there financial value in the opportunity, and is the management team capable? Are supply-and-demand economics working for or against the opportunity? I don't recommend gambling, but if you do, understand the odds, and don't gamble anything you are not willing to lose.

Imagine yourself as a finalist on Monty Hall's *Let's Make a Deal*. There are three doors from which you will choose—behind one is a car, and behind each of the other two, a goat. A choice is made; you have either chosen a car or a goat. The host immediately opens one of the unchosen doors to reveal a goat (the host never opens the door with the car). The host presents an option to switch doors or remain with your original choice. Quick analysis: there are two doors left to choose from. The car is behind one of the two doors. There are even odds that the car is behind the door you originally chose. This is random. There are no better odds whether you change or hold fast to your original choice; therefore, the decision is completely emotional—correct?

Hold your (emotional) horses! This is a perfect scenario for using reason (letting the charioteer lead). The car is behind one of the three doors. There is a one-in-three chance of choosing correctly with your first guess; you either choose correctly or you do not. Does the probability that the first choice is correct improve when more information is obtained (i.e., when the host opens a door to reveal a goat)?

Given that the car is behind one of three doors, and given that the contestant can choose any of the three doors, there are nine possible scenarios (Figure 28). Suppose the contestant first chooses Door 1. The car is either behind Door 1, 2, or 3 (scenario 1-1 represents the original choice of Door 1 with the car also behind Door 1, 1-2 represents the original choice of Door 1 with the car behind Door 2, and 1-3 represents the original choice of Door 1 with the car behind Door 3). Similarly, when the contestant first chooses Door 2, the car is either behind Door 1, 2, or 3 (scenarios 2-1, 2-2, or 2-3), and when the contestant first chooses Door 3, the car is either behind Door 1, 2, or 3 (scenarios 3-1, 3-2, or 3-3). When the contestant first chooses correctly (choosing the door behind which there is a car), the host opens either of the two remaining doors. For instance, when the car is behind Door 1 and the contestant chooses Door 1, the host can open

Door 2 or Door 3 to reveal a goat. In this scenario, if the contestant chooses to keep Door 1, he or she will win the car.

When the contestant chooses incorrectly, however, the host can open only one door to reveal a goat. As an example, if the contestant chooses Door 1, but the car is actually behind Door 2 (scenario 1-2) the host can open only Door 3 to reveal a goat. In this scenario, if the contestant remains with Door 1, he or she will lose, but if the contestant switches to Door 2, he or she will win. As another example, if the contestant chooses Door 1, but the car is actually behind Door 3 (scenario 1-3), the host can open only Door 2 to reveal a goat. In this scenario, if the contestant remains with Door 1, he or she will also lose, but if the contestant switches to Door 3, he or she will win. So, in effect, the contestant wins two out of three times by changing doors and only one of three times by remaining with his or her original decision. All nine scenarios and possible outcomes are detailed in Figure 28.

Scenario	Behind Door 1:	Behind Door 2:	Behind Door 3:	Contestant first chooses:	Host opens:	If the contestant changes doors, he or she:	If the contestant does not change doors, he or she:
1-1	Car	Goat	Goat		Door 2 or 3	Loses	Wins
1-2	Goat	Car	Goat	Door 1	Door 3	Wins	Loses
1-3	Goat	Goat	Car		Door 2	Wins	Loses
2-1	Car	Goat	Goat		Door 3	Wins	Loses
2-2	Goat	Car	Goat	Door 2	Door 1 or 3	Loses	Wins
2-3	Goat	Goat	Car		Door 1	Wins	Loses
3-1	Car	Goat	Goat		Door 2	Wins	Loses
3-2	Goat	Car	Goat	Door 3	Door 1	Wins	Loses
3-3	Goat	Goat	Car		Door 1 or 2	Loses	Wins
					Chances to win:	6 of 9 or 67%	3 of 9 or 33%

Figure 28: All possible scenarios of the Monty Hall problem

Considering all nine scenarios, the overall probabilities of winning are revealed. Interestingly, the one in three, or 33 percent, odds of choosing correctly with the first guess do not change at all with added information, but in only three of the nine scenarios does the contestant choose correctly with the first guess. In the remaining six of nine scenarios (when the initial guess is incorrect), the contestant will win if he or she changes doors. Thus, there is not a 50 percent but a 67 percent chance of winning by changing doors. Your first guess has a one-in-three chance of being correct and a two-in-three chance of being incorrect. The host reveals an incorrect answer, eliminating one of the two possibilities to land on a goat—so changing doors will result in a win six of nine times.

Emotionally, you will either win or lose. You may think, "I am lucky—my first choice is correct." Or you may fear the one in three chance of learning that you first chose correctly only to change your mind and subsequently lose. If you change your door selection, you will lose one of three times, but you don't have two more chances. Will reason win over emotion? Recall Shiv's analysis of neurologically impaired patients' versus "healthy" patients' investments, where loss aversion inhibited the healthy patients from achieving better returns (Refer to "Framework of Thought, Part III" in *VerAegis—Relationships*). In the same manner, loss aversion compels many contestants to stay with their first choice. What about you? The choice is yours to make— emotions or reason?

Infrequent events, such as buying a home or car, choosing a school or career, or picking a sport to play during a given season, do not usually require quick, on-the-spot decisions, so time is available for a more rigorous analysis. Many people adhere to the belief that one should listen solely to gut instincts because of the complexity of multivariable decisions, the ambiguity of non-quantifiable attributes such as peace, joy, happiness, security and so on, combined with the perceived burdens associated with evaluating so many variables, but in my experience, I have found that a more deliberate process yields better and more satisfying results.

In her sophomore year, my daughter, Teagan, was faced with the decision of either joining a gymnastics club in order to prepare for her high school gymnastics season or joining her high school track team. Her school was small, and she felt somewhat obligated to join the track team, if only so they would have more team members. She thought about her choices and finally decided to join the track team. Her main reason for choosing track was to enjoy the camaraderie of classmates versus belonging to a team composed of teammates she did not know as well. A couple days after her decision, I noticed that she was moping around (she claims she was not moping but simply contemplating her decision). She lamented that she was still unsure about her decision, but she still had not committed to her coach; so we had time to work together.

This was not a life-altering decision, but it was a great opportunity for Teagan to learn how to work through tough decisions. We agreed to use a simple but effective matrix decision process, which requires two lists. The first is a list of possible scenarios. The second is a list of desired results or attributes that will be used to rate each of the scenarios. Next, you need to choose two scales, one for rating how well each attribute impacts or relates to each scenario and the second to measure the relative importance (weight) of each attribute. I have found it useful to review both weighted and nonweighted results. I prefer to use a simple three scale rather than finer gradients of five, seven, or even ten, because, in my experience, the additional struggle and increased time requirement necessitated by additional rating options does not provide adequate return on investment. In fact, by choosing a scale with only three levels, with a significant difference in each level (e.g., a scale of 1-3-9 rather than 1-2-3), you are afforded the opportunity to drive more differentiation between your scenarios, and thus drive more quickly to a decision. It also affords the opportunity for a three-pass process: the first pass to determine the 9s, the second to identify 1s, and the third to fill all remaining blanks with 3s.

Teagan listed the desired results she wished to glean from participating in either gymnastics or track: personal enjoyment or gratification, camaraderie, environment, alignment with personal goals, and imagining whether she would be at ease with her decision in a few months. The next step was to assign a weight to each attribute. A weight of 1 means that attribute or desired result is optional (low importance), 3 is necessary, and 9 is vital (high importance). Teagan did not include any attributes that she felt were optional, so none were ranked a 1. She realized that her primary purpose for participating in sports was to learn, improve health and strength, and add variety to her workouts, so she assigned an importance of 9 to personal enjoyment. She rated all other attributes as necessary (3).

Next, Teagan applied the 1-3-9 scale to estimate the likelihood of attaining each desired outcome or attribute from each scenario. In other words, a rating of 1 for a given attribute-scenario combination would indicate that the given scenario had a particularly low likelihood of delivering the desired result, whereas a rating of 3 would have a midlevel likelihood, and a rating of 9, an excellent likelihood. During the rating process, I learned Teagan loved gymnastics but felt obligated to participate in track to help her classmates and coach. She felt that gymnastics had an excellent likelihood (9) of being gratifying, whereas track had only a medium chance (3). Recall that she considered personal enjoyment vital, and it thus had a weighting of 9. To determine the weighted scores (WS), Teagan simply multiplied the weight times the rating (W x R = WS): the weighted score for the likelihood of enjoying gymnastics was 9 x 9 = 81, but for track, it was 9 x 3 = 27 (Figure 29).

The sum of nonweighted scores was 33 for gymnastics and 21 for track. The difference of 12 is not small but perhaps not much greater than the margin of error for such an analysis. That is precisely the reason for reviewing weighted results, where differences in the most important attributes sway the decision more heavily. The sum of weighted scores was 153 for gymnastics and 81 for track. The difference of 72 is quite significant and favored participation in gymnastics, contrary to Teagan's original decision.

Option (Scenario) / Desired Result or Attribute	Weight	Gymnastics (March-Aug)	Track (Feb-May)	Comments
Personal enjoyment.		9	3	Loves gymnastics, feels obligated to participate in track.
Comradery: having close friends on the team.		3	9	Classmates on the track team; aquaintenances on gymnastics team.
Pleasant environment (inside/outside).		3	3	Gymnastics is inside. Track is outside which is good, but spring is often cold and wet in the northwest.
Personal goals and challenges.		9	3	Teagan had already established personal goals for gymnastics; track was more to help out the team.
In a few months (looking back) how do you think you will you feel about your decision?		9	3	She had made the decision to join the track; and seemed to be moping as a result.
		33	21	
Weight				
Personal enjoyment.	9	81	27	When tasked with weighing the relative importance of the attributes, Teagan ranked personal enjoyment of the sport as vital; comradery as important
Comradery: having close friends on the team.	3	9	27	Teagan was afraid to disappoint her friends classmates so chose track
Pleasant environment (inside/outside).	3	9	9	
Personal goals and challenges.	3	27	9	
In a few months (looking back) how do you think you will you feel about your decision?	3	27	9	
		153	81	

Figure 29: Weighted and nonweighted scores comparing the options for Teagan to participate in gymnastics or track

Teagan's initial emotional decision was based on her devotion to her classmates. She loved her friends and desired to be with them outside on the track. Without thinking more deeply, her devotion dominated her emotions and thoughts, but after deciding for track, she felt uneasy. Fortunately, she responded to her feelings and was open to additional analysis. We completed the assessment in about half an hour, using a simple Excel spreadsheet to arrive at a different conclusion. She decided to sign up for gymnastics, creating the opportunity to meet new friends and still have time during school hours to spend with her classmates. Teagan decided to wait a couple of days before making her "final" decision (neither deadline was pressing). She thought it best to see how she felt. I noticed that Teagan had the spring back in her step. One day passed, and then two, and then three before I asked how she felt about her decision. She smiled, lighting the room with her joy, and said, "Gymnastics is the right choice, Poppy!"

I have worked with teams to apply the same (or a similar) process to purchase multimillion-dollar semiconductor process equipment, to purchase training bikes, to select which elementary or high school to attend, to decide between job offers, and even to choose where to buy a house and which house to buy. This process facilitates decisions because it is simple, but even more so because the journey is as important as the destination. Discussing each scenario, the desired outcomes, the relative importance of selection criteria, and the final ratings is invaluable. Be true to those discussions. Use coordinated thinking. Don't belittle someone else's thoughts or feelings. Embrace the journey.

Consider the prospect of a couple (Kate and Ron, each thirty-something) who are considering buying a new home. Their first child, Jake, is three and a half, and their second, Amanda, eighteen months. Kate just decided to become a stay-at-home mom. Ron recently accepted a promotion at work, and, living in the city, he often bikes the short three miles to the office. Their lives together are pretty good, but the family of four has outgrown their small apartment. They contemplate options: buy a small condo or townhouse in the city, a slightly larger house in the suburbs, or an even larger house in the country, perhaps even with some land. They quickly decide to stay in the city. They are comfortable there and seem to be quite happy, but after a few months of searching, they experience the haunting feeling that they might be heading down the wrong path.

They decide to use the decision matrix process to help select where they should live. They agree to the following:

1. Discuss and list the options or scenarios (Figure 30).

2. Discuss and list the desired results or attributes that will be used to rate each scenario.

3. Assign a weight to each attribute. Kate and Ron's discussion of weights was eye-opening. See the comments in Figure 31.

4. Discuss and rate the correlation between each attribute and each scenario.

   a. First pass: Scenarios that have an excellent likelihood of delivering the desired result receive a 9 in the appropriate row or column.

   b. Second pass: Those scenarios that have a decidedly low likelihood of delivering the desired result receive a 1 in the appropriate row or column.

   c. Third pass: Score the remaining blanks with 3s.

5. Evaluate weighted and nonweighted results.

6. Discuss the results. If merited, make adjustments. Discuss the results again.

7. Wait a day or two. Revisit the decision. How do they feel? What do their guts say?

Upon completing their first pass (nonweighted), Ron and Kate were surprised to find that purchasing a home in the city, though originally their first choice, was now dead last. They were equally surprised to find that the suburban and rural locations were practically in a dead heat, and pleasantly surprised to find that only one of the attributes (environment) offered no differentiation among the three scenarios (Figure 30).

They continued the process by assigning relative importance (weights) to each attribute. Both were determined to designate a portion of the attributes as vital (9) and others as optional (1). They agreed that if one of the two thought an attribute was vital, they would document the reasoning in the comment column and score that attribute as a 9 rather than debate the details. The process went smoothly, the

Desired Result or Attribute	Small Expensive City Home	Fair Sized Suburban Home	Large Rural Home	Comments
Affordability-debt to income ratio	3	9	9	The city home that fits our space requirements is over twice as expensive.
Safety and crime rate	3	9	9	City streets are less conducive for kids to play in the immediate neighborhood.
Proximity to work (commute time)	9	3	1	Not clear that the city commute will be much better when driving, but more access to public transportation.
Proximity to schools	3	3	1	Further drive, but less congestion in suburban and rural areas.
Proximity to stores	9	9	1	
Proximity to friends and family	3	3	1	
Proximity to fire & police departments, EMS, and hospitals.	9	9	1	Response time in urban area matched city. Rural was much longer.
Comfort and likability	3	9	9	
Guest room	1	3	9	City home-guest will sleep on pull out couch. Urban-shared guest and game room. Rural-full extra room with bathroom.
Size of yard	1	3	9	
Size of garage	1	3	9	
View	1	3	9	
Environment: City-Urban-Rural	3	3	3	Access to social activity vs. nature and wilderness.
	49	69	71	

Figure 30: Nonweighted decision matrix—where to purchase a home?

discussion was fruitful, and they agreed to rank affordability; safety; proximity to work; proximity to schools; proximity to fire, police, and other emergency services; and comfort/likability as vital. Next they determined which attributes were truly optional: guest room and view. All others they rated as 3, or necessary (Figure 31).

The surprises continued! Purchasing a smaller home in the city was now rated nearly the same as purchasing a large rural home. The clear winner was the scenario in which they purchased a decent-sized suburban home. Both were happy with the process and felt pretty good about the decision. Still at peace with the decision a few days later, they notified their real estate agent of their change in plans.

Desired Result or Characteristic	Weight	Small Expensive City Home	Fair Sized Suburban Home	Large Rural Home	Comments
Affordability-debt to income ratio	9	27	81	81	With likelihood of a layoff within the next 5 years; affordability deemed vital.
Safety and crime rate	9	27	81	81	Vital for quality of life.
Proximity to work (commute time)	9	81	27	9	Vital for quality of life.
Proximity to schools	9	27	27	9	Vital for quality of life.
Proximity to stores	3	27	27	3	Important, but not vital. Note in the city we will have to walk more; so will need to carry groceries.
Proximity to friends and family	3	9	9	3	Important, but not vital We can drive a little longer to meet with friends and family
Proximity to fire & police departments, EMS, and hospitals.	9	81	81	9	A rapid response is vital when needed.
Comfort and likability	9	27	81	81	Feeling at ease in our home is vital.
Guest room	1	1	3	9	Guest room deemed optional.
Size of yard	3	3	9	27	Decent yard, important, but not vital.
Size of garage	3	3	9	27	Important, but not vital.
View	1	1	3	9	View beyond our yard is optional.
Environment: City-Urban-Rural	3	9	9	9	Important, but not vital. Various environments have different benefits...keep at neutral.
		323	447	357	

Figure 31: Weighted decision matrix—where to purchase a home?

Ron and Kate had nearly made a completely emotional decision, but fortunately, by continually monitoring their emotions, they came to the realization that living in the city might not be the best choice for them. They learned more about each other during the decision-matrix process. They "held their horses at bay," applied reason, and arrived at a mutually beneficial decision. Once decided, they contemplated both the process and the new plan, once again consulting their gut instincts. They continued to feel good about their new choice and so moved forward.

Unique Situations Requiring New Solutions

New solutions require creative thinking. They are sometimes conceived randomly and sometimes the result of deliberate thought processes. Random, serendipitous ideas are wonderful but not necessarily reliable in their timing, so when faced with a problem that requires a new solution, it is preferable to rely on a process rather than chance. We admire and at times are in awe of exceptionally talented and creative individuals, but is it possible that two (or more) minds are better than one when attempting to find a new solution?

In the 1970s, the US government commissioned a study to determine the answer. Thirty experts participated in the study. Each expert was requested to independently review the same intelligence data and then predict enemy-troop movement. The experts submitted their independent reports to the commission, who compiled and analyzed the data. Each expert was then afforded the opportunity to review and assimilate the twenty-nine reports from his or her peers before submitting a revised report. Note that the twenty-nine peer reports contained no new data—only differing interpretations of original data.

The commission reviewed the original and revised predictions and compared them with actual troop movements, which were segmented into one hundred "elements." The experts' average original score, achieved independently, was a mere seven correct elements. However, the average accuracy of the revised reports was seventy-nine correct elements; on average, each expert's ability to predict a solution improved over eleven times without any additional data (Spool 2004), suggesting that there are indeed some situations where two (or thirty) minds are better than one. This result is based on the premises that no one of us knows more than all of us and that synergy is possible only when differences occur.

Brainstorming is a group technique used to stimulate creative thinking by allowing unfettered and spontaneous sharing of ideas. During traditional brainstorming, a problem is posed to the group by a facilitator, and as ideas begin to flow, a scribe attempts to capture the ideas in writing, perhaps on a whiteboard or projected screen. The team is given a set of guidelines to abide by, which usually includes the following:

1) There are no dumb ideas; if it comes to your mind, blurt it out. Others may benefit from your thoughts.

2) The brainstorm session is designed to exercise creative thinking; do not criticize others' ideas.

3) Build on ideas as they are shared. Synergize in real time.

4) Go for quantity, not quality (remember, no idea is considered a bad idea).

These sessions can be fun and engaging. However, it often happens that 20 percent of the participants dominate the conversation, limiting ideas from more introverted team members.

A solution I prefer is a twist on brainstorming, often referred to as a silent brainstorm, an affinity process, or a KJ method (Jiro Kawakita devised a similar process in the 1960s). In the standard KJ method, ideas are recorded on note cards or sticky notes by each participant. The notes are posted on a wall, and as participants notice similarities between ideas, the notes are gathered into groups. Once the sorting has been completed and all cards are repositioned, theme statements are generated for each group. Each team member has an equal number of "votes" (usually stickers), and they all proceed to vote for which theme is the best, most important, or most urgent, depending on the original problem statement. The themes are then ranked according to the highest number of votes.

The silent brainstorm process is effective and relatively quick. In my experience, adding an additional step is extremely helpful: the notes are gathered and read aloud by the facilitator prior to being posted on the wall. This step takes longer, but it offers several upsides. When read, the meaning and intent of some of the ideas are immediately understood, while for others, this is not the case. Misunderstood notes cause difficulty during the sorting process, and often side discussions ignite as team members try to ascertain meaning. By reading each idea aloud, the idea can be clarified through group discussion until there is a general consensus that the idea is understood. Another advantage of this process is that, similar to a more traditional brainstorming process, the participants are allowed to build on ideas by submitting additional notes during the reading session. Some of the best ideas I have encountered were new submissions generated while the ideas were being discussed and refined.

The steps for the modified silent brainstorm are as follows:

Step 1: Clearly define and state the purpose (desired result) of the brainstorm session.

What problem needs to be resolved or solution created, for whom, and by when? What are the key performance metrics that need to be improved?

As an example, the objective may be "Our objective is to develop a new product (SureFire) that addresses the need to provide higher efficiency (30 percent reduced power consumption) to the home heating and air-conditioning market. In meeting the new performance metrics (refer to our more detailed product requirements sheet), we will improve market share in our existing markets and gain access to emerging market needs: (1) lower cost of ownership, (2) increased customer satisfaction via improved reliability and reduced size, and (3) time to market of eighteen (or fewer) months."

Step 2: Form the team and organize the brainstorm session.

Determine who will facilitate the brainstorming process. Identify the champion (the person who most desires a solution, and usually the person who helped most to define the desired results in the first step). Invite key stakeholders and experts in relevant disciplines to develop a solution. The ideal group size is six to eight, but I have seen this process work with twelve or more participants—though with each additional person, more time is required.

Step 3: Silently brainstorm.

Once the purpose is well understood and all questions are answered, each participant silently writes his or her ideas on note cards or sticky notes—one idea per note card. The author's name is not included.

Step 4: Confirm understanding—refine and build on ideas.

Each participant submits his or her notes to the facilitator. The facilitator reviews the notes with each participant as they are submitted to ensure legibility. When all ideas are turned in, the facilitator reads each aloud and refines the wording as necessary until there is general consensus that the meaning and intent of the idea is well understood. Some ideas require complete rewrites, while others need little or no editing. Participants are invited to build on any idea, if so inspired, by submitting additional notes during the reading session.

Step 5: Place the ideas on the wall and sort them into groups with common themes.

The notes are posted on a wall. Participants roam the room, searching for similarities among the posted ideas. The cards are repositioned into groups that seem to have common themes. All team members are encouraged to participate in the grouping. Several notes may be repositioned by different members to different groups. I have not witnessed any conflict, and in one case, when two team members each strongly believed one note belonged in two different groups, they created a duplicate to resolve the issue.

Step 6: Develop theme statements.

Once the sorting has been completed and all cards are repositioned, theme statements are generated for each grouping. The team members are divided into a number of groups matching the number of themes (if there are four groupings and twelve team members, form four groups of three). Each group develops a theme statement for its grouping of ideas. The groups then rotate until they have reviewed each of the other groups and had an opportunity to edit each theme. The theme statements are read aloud and refined until all the groups are satisfied that the theme adequately represents the individual ideas.

Step 7: Vote and rank.

Each team member is allocated an equal number of "votes" (usually stickers). Each is free to vote as he or she prefers on which theme is the best, most important, or most urgent, depending on the original problem statement. Team members may use all their votes for one theme or spread them around, depending solely on their preference. The themes are then ranked according to the number of votes—the more votes, the higher the priority.

Step 8: Publish results.

Publish (or post) the project objectives and a summary, including each of the major themes developed. Also include a detailed list in which all the ideas are listed under their major themes. Include the names of the team members, facilitator, and champion.

Effective Decision Making Summarized

Effective decisions are most often made by applying a combination of reason and emotion. Determine when the decision needs to be made, and if there is no benefit to an early decision, wait as long as possible to gather more information or to analyze your emotions between the time you decide and the time you commit. In the heat of the moment, remember that emotional thinking is essential but most often should not be given priority. Emotions are best employed in situations with somewhat predictable patterns that require a quick decision and do not afford the luxury of detailed analysis. When time permits, compile your options and the standards by which the decision will be made. If at all possible, work with others to gain a balanced perspective. Working with others may help avoid a tendency to convince ourselves that bad decisions are not really so bad. Such a balanced perspective is also extremely beneficial when thinking creatively, and when approached synergistically, a combination of silent and vocal brainstorming is often quite effective.

Recall that individual paradigms are as much based in our history as they are in actual reality. We see the world through our experientially formed lenses. Be wary of marketers and a host of others who are paid to sway our views, emotions and decisions; they are paid to sway the way we see the world and thus influence our decisions. Working with others may help us avoid the targeted subliminal messages of professional marketers. Finally, be cautious in gain-or-loss situations, which play on emotions. When confident in our individual and group decision-making processes, we will be better able to effectively influence our future and the future of the teams to which we belong!

Effective Meetings and Communication

Have you ever been to a meeting that just didn't seem to work? Did people seem to be gathered together, but the purpose was unknown or elusive? Have you been to a meeting that seemed like it would never end, and when it finally did end, your relief was overshadowed by the feeling that you and your colleagues had just wasted valuable time?

On the contrary, have you been to a meeting where everything seemed to click? Item after item was discussed, decisions made, and actions reviewed. The meeting ended on time, and the team members left energized, with plenty to accomplish prior to meeting again.

What were the differences between the two scenarios? Why was one meeting such a success and the other a drain on resources and morale? Typically, meetings are a success or failure long before they start: preparation is key. Organize in advance.

Define the specific purpose or objective of the meeting. The agenda should be "built" in a manner that ensures the objective will be attained. The purpose, agenda, and meeting guidelines should be published in advance of the meeting. Each agenda item should include an owner, a summary of the desired results to be attained during that portion of the meeting, and the allotted time. The allotted time and desired results are included so that if the desired results are attained in less than the allotted time, the facilitator can move to the next agenda item, but if the desired results are not attained in the allotted time, an action should be documented to follow up with the owner to determine how best to attain the desired outcome.

Setting guidelines in advance establishes expectations and requires only a short time at the onset of the meeting to confirm the guidelines are acceptable, and if not, to make any adjustments deemed necessary. Typical guidelines include starting on time, restating the purpose, staying on agenda, staying on topic, moving on once desired results are attained, cooperating and applying parallel thinking techniques, listening to understand, asking direct questions, recording answers, recording action items, not taking phone calls unless absolutely necessary, notifying meeting organizers in advance if a "call-in" is necessary or if you will send a rep because you are unable to attend, and, for extended meetings, scheduling breaks every ninety minutes or so. Avoid texting or sending e-mail during a meeting; even if your participation is not required in the meeting, you will be more productive elsewhere and less distracting to those who are required to participate.

When facilitating the meeting, recall parallel thinking techniques. Start the meeting by restating the type of meeting, the purpose, and the agenda. Confirm the guidelines and assign a timekeeper. During presentations and data reviews, remind the audience that it is crucial to analyze the available data in terms of its completeness and accuracy, with the intent that the data will illuminate a path forward. Optimistic thinking is used to define the value of the opportunity or solution and create proposals, depending on the data and the type of meeting. If appropriate, the team should be invited to poke and prod the data so that flaws are brought to the surface. Then creative thinking should be applied in order to define next steps, improve the data, and fill any existing gaps. Near the end of the meeting, the facilitator may request the team to comment on how they feel regarding the outcomes: Do they feel the direction is correct? Do they feel sufficient analysis has been employed? Were any concerns overlooked? Finally, the meeting should be concluded with a quick summary of any decisions and open action items.

In my experience, most meetings fall into one of six general categories: (1) reporting and information sharing; (2) decision making and steering; (3) working and problem solving; (4) creative brainstorming; (5) training and education; and (6) team building, celebration, or entertainment.

Reporting and Information Sharing

Information-sharing (report-out) meetings are often attended by teams of six or more people, who share status updates among themselves. These meetings are commonplace in the workforce and run the risk of becoming bogged down and boring. Information is shared via many formats, including presentations, spreadsheets, Gantt charts and action boards. Exception management, the ability to quickly probe success and pass over items that are on target—drilling briefly into areas of risk or failure—is key to keeping these meetings "fresh." When a large problem that merits more discussion surfaces, a follow-up decision-making and steering meeting should be scheduled with six or fewer people.

Decision Making and Steering

It is a mistake to assume that all decisions are only made in decision-making and steering meetings. On the contrary, these meetings are devoted solely to big decisions or changes in direction that require input from many individuals in order to achieve synergy. These meetings can be touchy, especially if the steering is meant to restructure a troubled project. Additionally, the decision-making process needs to be clear (unilateral, subgroup, majority rule, or consensus—refer to Making Good Decisions Is Key to Being Effective). The objective and agendas needs to be clearly stated: What decisions need to be made and what barriers need to be overcome? Participants need to prepare in advance so that they have the necessary data to present and facilitate decisions, but precautions need to be taken so that each participant maintains an open mind. Preconceived notions and decisions are often difficult to overcome and have the tendency to derail meetings if allowed to get out of control. Note that decision making can be a synergistic process when creative thinking processes are applied. If the desired result is consensus around a decision or new path, the leader, with lack of consensus, is faced with two options: (1) make the call if adequate data has been reviewed and the schedule mandates a decision, or (2) reschedule, if time permits, after defining additional data required to arrive at a decision and assigning responsibilities to those who need to gather the data.

Working and Problem Solving

To be most effective, working sessions should be limited to two to six participants. The purpose and agenda should be clearly stated. Each participant should know in advance what material and data he or she is responsible for sharing. The appropriate tools should be available to do the job (computers, whiteboards, dry-erase pens, Post-it notes, projectors, etc.).The team should use parallel thinking techniques to avoid conflict and increase the possibility of synergy.

Brainstorming

Meetings whose purpose is to find new, innovative solutions are meant to be fertile and exciting. Participants should be encouraged and feel free to offer ideas. Refer to "Unique Solutions Requiring New Solutions" in "Making Good Decisions Is Key to Being Effective."

Training and Education

The trainer or educator needs to be well prepared. Training sessions need to move at a pace facilitating understanding while maintaining interest in order to be effective. Group participation is essential. Control is also essential to ensure the desired material is adequately covered, yet control needs to be balanced with the desire to encourage open, two-way communication. The facilitator should be adept at guiding parallel thinking techniques to avoid conflict and increase the possibility of synergy.

Team Building, Celebration, and Entertainment

Also known as parties, these meetings are too often overlooked. Take time to stop and smell the roses. Celebrate success and   positive results, but don't forget to plan these meetings as well. I have learned (the hard way) that praise for one person is often a jab to another. In other words, if one team member is singled out for praise, other team members may be resentful. Take care to acknowledge teamwork and exemplary performance in a manner that does more good than harm.

Effective Communication

Has anyone—a parent, teacher, or supervisor—ever stated to you, "I don't understand you! You just don't listen!"? Perhaps you looked at them quizzically, so they repeated themselves a few more times for emphasis. Ironically, for someone to understand another, the key is not to talk but to listen. Perhaps those people should have stated, "I don't understand you! I just don't listen!"

Listening is a skill that must be honed by practice. Many people listen with the intent to respond rather than understand—listening intently to a point and then drifting in thought and contemplating how to counter what they have heard. In order to understand, one must employ ears, eyes, and, most importantly, heart. With ears, ascertain another's meaning listening not just to their words but also to their tone and emphasis. With the eyes, search for visual cues like body language, facial expressions, perspiration, fidgeting, and other signs of stress, calm, fear, anger, or other emotions. With the heart, detect sincerity: Does this person mean what he or she is saying? The heart is also the key to your own intent: do you intend to dominate, win, or compete, or to genuinely understand and care? Remember that understanding is to relationships what air is to life! Your heart fashions your attitude, which in turn directs your actions.

It is helpful to communicate your intent to seek understanding. Tell the people with whom you're speaking that you will ask clarifying questions and restate what you have learned until they are satisfied that you truly understand their position. It may be useful to establish guidelines: for example, reach understanding first and then, if possible, agreement. The goal is mutual understanding before agreement, and your intent is to understand before being understood. In my experience, most people will be happy to be understood prior to seeking to understand, but try not to force the issue if they wish to understand first.

Asking Effective Questions

Asking questions effectively and asking effective questions are invaluable skills when trying to gain understanding. Start with your intent. For example, "Jane, I would like to better understand what you intend to accomplish, and if it is okay, I'd like to ask some questions to make sure I understand your motivation, desired results, and timeline. Once I'm able to restate your position to your satisfaction, we will reverse the process. I will happily respond to your questions until we've agreed that you adequately understand our (or my) needs. Then together, we can plan next steps and begin to develop a plan to move forward. How does that sound?"

Once given the green light to begin a question-and-answer session, follow a few guidelines. Ask one question at a time, and wait for the answer. When people break eye contact, looking up or down, they are often searching for the correct words. Don't rush them; allow ample "quiet time" for them to search for and find answers. Repeat the answer in your own words. Confirm understanding. Ask clarifying questions until they confirm that you have understood their message.

Show appreciation (verbally and nonverbally) before moving to your next question. Smile and say, "Thanks, Jane. I feel I am starting to see the picture more clearly now." People are more willing to answer additional questions when they feel their input is appreciated and useful. Use "how" or "what" questions rather than "why" questions, unless, of course, attempting to determine the root cause of a problem; then employ the five whys (see "A Horse by Any Other Name"). Be attentive to emotions, however, when using "why" questions, for they tend to evoke feelings of defensiveness and responses that justify rather than clarify. At times, a preferred approach may be to ask, "How did that happen?" or "What caused that to occur?" rather than, "Why did that happen?"

Finally, be alert. Don't talk too much; even when asking questions, it is possible to dominate the conversation. As a rule of thumb, when listening, the person to whom you are listening should speak two to three times as much as you do. In other words, he or she should speak at least ten of every fifteen minutes.

In order to facilitate dialogue, employ short, probing questions that elicit detailed responses. Then observe and listen. Be receptive. Ask clarifying questions like the following: Can you help me understand how this relates to our discussion? If I understand correctly, you intend to...Is that right? How does this compare to our historical understanding? Is there more? Don't be afraid to question underlying assumptions: What has led to that assumption [or conclusion]? What could we assume instead? Dive into data and evidence: Have you observed this phenomenon? What do you think causes this to happen? How did you arrive at that conclusion? Can you think of any analogies that are already well understood? Analyze perspectives using optimistic and critical thinking: Why do you think this is important? What is another way to look at this? Have you considered alternative causes? What are the benefits? Are there additional upsides? Who are the recipients of the benefits? What can possibly go wrong? What is the counterargument against moving forward with this idea? What are the downsides?

Finally, when it is your turn to answer the questions, don't be afraid to ask clarifying questions to ensure understanding of the question itself: Can you help me understand the purpose of this question? What are you hoping to understand? What do you mean by...?

Proactive Attitude

Be wary of reactive language and attitudes during question-and-answer sessions. Speakers need to understand that they portray themselves as victims when using reactive language. Listeners need to be wary of further "victimizing" a reactive speaker, as cornering any victim can lead to volatile situations. Reactive language is a quick ticket to the crazy cycle. Instead, learn to employ proactive attitudes and language.

During question-and-answer sessions, the questioned might become defensive and emotional, thus reverting to reactive language. The proactive questioner should reflect emotions and attempt to ease the situation before continuing. The questioned should also strive to remain proactive. When asked, "What can you do about this?" rather than blurting out, "There's nothing I can do!" he or she should instead reply, "Let's look at our alternatives. As I see it, we have [x number] of scenarios to consider. First…"

Be cautious not to feel like, "That's just the way I am." Instead believe, "I will choose a different approach." If disturbed by a question, think, "I have the freedom, the power and responsibility to choose my response. I am aware of my emotions, but they do not control my response" rather than, "He [or she] is making me so angry, and my emotions control my response!" Remember that you don't "have to do something…"; instead you will choose an appropriate response, balancing the courage to stand for your beliefs and convictions with consideration for the beliefs and convictions of others. Instead of "I can't," use "I choose." Replace "I must" with "I prefer" and "I expect" with "I desire." Treat others as if they are proactive. For example, replace the question "Why didn't you consider this or that?" with "What did you determine when you considered this or that?" When treated as though they are proactive, our family members, friends and colleagues are more likely to respond proactively, which leads to far more satisfying and effective communication.

Get Results, Appraise Performance, and Celebrate Success

Our performance is continuously critiqued, just as we continuously critique the performance of others. Self-evaluation and an open mind are prerequisites to self-improvement and increased self-awareness. Self-awareness and open communication are fundamental to preventing most surprises when faced with a critique of our performance. Lack of communication, misaligned expectations, over- or underempowerment, and poor self-awareness can all result in "surprising" performance reviews, whether informal reviews by friends and family or formal reviews at school or work.

When self-aware and proactive, individuals continuously evaluate their status and circumstances. How do you view the world? Do you face problems head-on or rely on others? Do you have an adequate understanding of priorities and act accordingly, putting top priorities first? Do you take time to plan and schedule? Are you on top of life, working on important projects before they become urgent, or are you being pushed along like a snowball in an avalanche, only finding time to work on one emergency after another? Are goals

> **If you could kick the person in the pants responsible for most of your trouble, you wouldn't sit for a month.**
> Theodore Roosevelt

continuously achieved with mutual benefit for others or seldom achieved as desired? With continuous self-evaluation comes the opportunity to self-adjust and course correct.

Similarly, open communication with supervisors and peers is an excellent means to determine whether or not your performance is on track. Don't wait for yearly reviews to ascertain whether you are delivering satisfactory or exemplary results. When a task is completed, simply ask, "Did this meet your desired results? Is there anything else you need or something you would like done differently?" Follow through. If challenges are outpaced by increased knowledge and skills, you may begin to feel bored. On the other hand, if challenges outpace capabilities, you may feel overwhelmed. Don't wait for someone else to notice if you are over- or underempowered; be proactive and address the issue with your supervisor. If your organization cannot accommodate your needs, find one that can.

The crux of the matter is that someone will eventually evaluate your effectiveness (either formally or informally), so it is better to be prepared and manage the process along the way rather than wait for another's timing. Most performance evaluations (formal and informal) are based on both the results delivered and how they were completed. Recall that effectiveness requires the integrity to act on priorities in a manner that assures that one obtains the desired results repeatedly.

> **However beautiful the strategy, you should occasionally look at the results.**
>
> Winston Churchill

Effectiveness requires character and competence. In your gut, you already know whether or not you are effective. Others, too, are aware. Don't attempt to fool yourself; no one else is fooled. An appraisal process is a means to formalize and quantify these instinctive understandings.

There is not one correct way to evaluate performance. In my experience, 360-degree reviews, which are completed by supervisors, peers, and, if applicable, subordinates, provide the most benefit. I have found that a simple process is far more effective than the "standard" process's multipage novellas, pontificating point after point, and infinitely more effective than withholding reviews altogether. Whether 360 degrees or not, a simple process minimizes bureaucracy, standardizes format, provides a common metric for all, and, once completed, requires only a concise summary statement. Refer to Figure 32, which illustrates the results of a rating and ranking process for a small ten-person high-tech start-up. Each individual is rated for competence and character, and then the scores are compiled into one spreadsheet to enable ranking among the ten employees.

Competence is a measure of one's ability to perform the job at hand; it is a combination of knowledge (facts and information required to deliver results, gained through experience and education) and skill or know-how (physical and mental dexterity gained through natural gifts, experience, and training). Character is a measure of how one approaches life, or more specifically, how one approaches the job for which he or she is being appraised; it is the aggregate of features like judgment, focus, discernment, trust, integrity, energy, self-motivation, and disposition. Character is born of your spirit.

The major categories used to measure character at this small startup were judgment (focus), trust (integrity), energy, and disposition (Figure 32). Weights were used to identify the most important metrics. In this example, competence, judgment, and integrity each had a weight of 25 percent, whereas energy was weighted at 15 percent, and disposition, at 10 percent. This team relied on each person to be technically competent in their area of responsiblity in order to succeed. The team was small and "flat" (meaning all of the team members reported to the founder, without any other formal organizational structure). Each person needed to know what was required and how to deliver. Each person also needed to understand the big picture well enough to be able to determine the correct course of action and prioritize accordingly. Finally, each team member needed to do the right thing even when no one else was looking, and just as importantly, the team required everyone to have the candor to respectfully raise issues even when doing so was uncomfortable. Each person received a score of either 10 (excels), 3 (on target), or 1 (missed expectations). Note, a max rating of 10 was used rather than 9 in order to enable a max score of 100. An alternate scale provides more gradual delineation and is often employed in other contexts: 1 (strongly misses), 2 (somewhat misses), 3 (on target), 4 (somewhat excels), and 5 (strongly excels).

Performance Rating and Ranking Process

	Assessment Criteria	Weight	Must haves:	P01	P02	P03	P04	P05	P06	P07	P08	P09	P10
Competence	Technical expertise (know what) and skills (know how) required to deliver desired results.	25%	Must have	10	3	3	10	10	3	10	10	10	1
Character		75%											
Judgment & Focus:	Discerning, alert, able to dive deep, understands the big picture, and spends time on the top priorities. Knows the 'right thing' to do.	25%	Must have	3	10	10	3	10	3	1	10	10	3
Trust-Integrity:	Does the 'right thing' even when nobody's looking. Respectfully candid–open.	25%	Must have	10	10	10	3	10	3	1	10	10	3
Energy:	Proactive, driven, self-motivated and enthusiastic.	15%		10	3	3	3	1	3	1	10	3	3
Disposition:	Ability to effectively work with others.	10%		10	3	10	3	1	3	1	3	10	3
	Not Weighted			43	29	36	22	32	15	14	43	43	13
	Weighted			8.3	6.5	7.2	4.8	7.8	3.0	3.3	9.3	9.0	2.5
	Weighted Score			83%	65%	72%	48%	78%	30%	33%	93%	90%	25%

Figure 32: Performance (character and competence) rating process

The scores for each employee were ranked from high to low and then displayed graphically (Figure 33). Borrowing from former General Electric CEO and chairman Jack Welch's ranking process, the team of ten was divided into three categories: the top 20 percent (employees P08 and P09), the vital 70 percent, and the bottom 10 percent (employee P10). Armed with the ratings and rankings, the company created actions and plans for each employee (Figure 34).

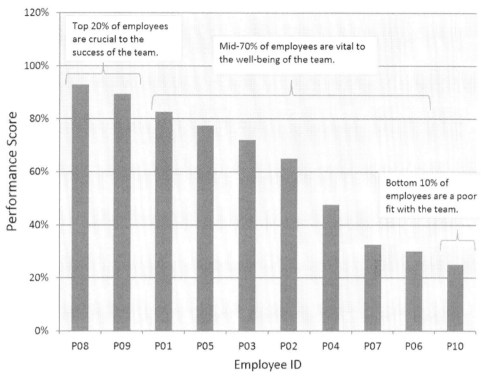

Figure 33: Graphical representation of performance rating score versus employee ID, ranked from high to low score

In general, the top performers in an organization are deemed crucial to the ongoing success of the company and need to be nurtured to grow and to continue delivering exemplary results and differentiation from competitors. The vital 70 percent are the heart and soul of the organization, also vital to getting things done, and must be cherished accordingly. Just as importantly, the bottom 10 percent do not fit in the organization, and so, changes are required. If ignored and allowed to continually miss expectations, the underperformer (or underperformers) may become a cancer, spreading discontent and disloyalty.

In our example of a small ten-person team, only one truly fell in the bottom 10 percent, but upon reviewing the details, it was determined

ID	Score	Rank	Actions/Comments	Revised Rank
P08	93%	Top 20	Nurture and incentivize to ensure he continues to be a strong team player.	Top 20
P09	90%	Top 20	Nurture and incentivize to ensure her drive does not drop.	Top 20
P01	83%	Vital 70	Cherish as part of the vital 70 or determine if coaching will move P1 to top 20.	Vital 70
P05	78%	Vital 70	Cherish as vital 70, but closely monitor **RESULTS**, and coach to improve drive and enthusiasm as necessary.	Vital 70
P03	72%	Vital 70	Cherish as vital 70. Provide job-specific training to improve expertise.	Vital 70
P04	48%	Vital 70	Cherish as vital 70. Provide soft-skill training to improve ability to understand the big picture and focus on top priorities	Vital 70
P02	65%	Vital 70	Cherish as vital 70. Provide job specific training to improve expertise.	Vital 70
P06	30%	Vital 70	Cherish as vital 70. Provide job specific training to improve expertise.	Vital 70
P07	33%	Vital 70	Scored in the low end of the vital 70; however, given the misses in two must have areas (Judgment and Integrity), move to bottom 10 and terminate at-will employment.	Bottom 10
P10	25%	Bottom 10	If there is a position inside the company that matches P10's expertise and skills move accordingly and coach into vital 70. Otherwise, provide outplacement assistance	Bottom 10

Figure 34: Ranking process and associated management actions

that in fact, two employees did not "fit" the team. Employee P07 was ranked highly for competence and scored in the low end of the vital 70 percent but missed expectations on all character metrics: judgment, integrity, energy, and disposition. Missing one or two of the character traits could be acceptable—but not all. Note that employee P05 (Paul), who excels in competence, judgment, and integrity, also ranked low for energy and disposition (often standoffish and grumpy). However, Paul capitalized on his combination of expertise and "laziness" to create solutions to problems that were ingeniously simple to reproduce. You see, his low energy is a big motivator to find the easiest way possible to accomplish a task. It turns out that the easiest way was usually the fastest and least costly as well. The team appreciated his contribution and made him aware of his nonsocial tendencies. Paul understood and appreciated the feedback. Paul was firmly in the vital 70. The team could not, however, tolerate the situation with employee P07, and so terminated at-will employment.

Meanwhile, P10, who was on target for all character traits but missed competence expectations, posed a different dilemma. This person worked well with the team, was trusted, and had solid judgment but clearly did not possess adequate knowledge and skills to perform the job. Three choices were available: find a suitable position matched to P10's skill sets within the organization; if time permits and P10 is motivated to learn, provide suitable training and education for the current position; or provide outplacement support to find a suitable position outside the organization.

The next step of the appraisal was to provide for each employee a concise statement of performance, including key contributions; expertise ratings, along with a brief description of how well their expertise and skills matched the requirements of their positions; and detailed character ratings. If the review process included peers and subordinates, each individual would receive information parsed into three categories (their supervisor, a group of peers, and a group of subordinates, unless any group has fewer than three participants, then peers and subordinates can be combined). Finally, personal development plans would be agreed on and entered into the MBO system as SMART goals (see "Set and Achieve Goals").

Finally, the team would take time to celebrate and reward success, acknowledging sound performance and results. Positive feedback is a powerful motivator. In general, people like (and need) to know that what they do matters.

Contribute: Sow a Service—Reap a Spirit

Be of service. It is not all about you. Don't carve out small portions of your life to be of service, rather—help others in all that you do. Build your house on rock, not sand. Be a stable influence. Organizations, teams, families, and individuals change. Either manage the change riding a wave of success and enjoyment, or be swept along in a stream of anxiety and confusion.

Adopt a healthy attitude of pragmatic optimism. Find your way based on data, facts, and feelings. Act with foresight, sound judgment, integrity, and a healthy spirit. Think effectively. Communicate effectively. Use the right "tool" for the job. Capitalize on your innate motivation and instincts. Continually self-assess and learn to self-correct, but perhaps just as importantly, learn to celebrate and enjoy success—not only your success but the success of others.

> **Be of service. Whether you make yourself available to a friend or co-worker, or you make time every month to do volunteer work, there is nothing that harvests more of a feeling of empowerment than being of service to someone in need.**
>
> Gillian Anderson

Make a contribution. At home. At work. In your community. Enjoy being of service and in doing so inspire a contribution and enjoy the success of others. Make the world a better place, and learn to be of sound character. Yes, contribution in all you do—inspire others and learn to be of good spirit!

Afterword

Once again, visualize life as a three-legged stool. One leg represents the health of your relationships, the next the impact of your contributions (negative or positive), and the final, the health of your spirit. We have invested time to better understand the importance of our contribution to our overall effectiveness, our relationships, and the health of our spirit. We investigated tools and learned techniques to help us to work smarter not harder. We learned how to better manage our finances and our time. We gained a deeper understanding of decision making, parallel thinking processes and the need to eliminate emotional debt. We established a process to set boundaries that allow us the freedom to think creatively about our contributions while balancing our time so that we do not neglect relationships or ourselves. We learned that through our contributions and effective communication we can positively impact others, inspiring them to "pay it forward." What better way is there to leave a legacy? In Book 1, we reviewed the value of relationships, and in Book 3, we will delve into spirit.

- Book 1 *VerAegis—Relationships*: Live your life. Touch another.
- Book 2 *VerAegis—Contribution*: Make a difference. Inspire another.
- Book 3 *VerAegis—Spirit*: Kindle your spirit. Ignite another.

VerAegis—The Legacy Series illuminates these three strands that are interwoven throughout our lives. We each *will* leave a legacy; and it is within our power and responsibility to leave the legacy we desire. I hope you enjoyed reading *VerAegis—Contribution*. I hope you marked it up and will refer back to it as you strive to balance your contribution with your relationships and your spirit. I

> **Though one may be overpowered, two can defend themselves. A cord of three strands is not quickly broken.**
> Ecclesiastes 4:12 (NIV)

also hope that you will find books 1 and 3 to be just as fulfilling. As a rope of three interwoven strands is not easily broken, there is synergy between these three books. Read on. Orchestrate your destiny.

Acknowledgements

- Sheri, Teagan, and Jimmy
- My dad (may he rest in peace), mom, stepdad, sisters, nieces, nephews, and all my in-laws
- Friends, colleagues, teachers, professors, and mentors

Thank you for your love and support. You have meant so much to me and have taught me more than I can express. Please accept my apologies for all the times I have fallen short of the ideals described in this book! I hope that by writing this book, I will have improved and expanded my comfort zone as I continue my efforts to become more effective and live a more balanced life.

Sheri, Teagan, Dawne, Mom, George, Jimmy, and McKenna, thank you for reading, editing, and suggesting improvements. *VerAegis* is better as a result.

Maria, Savannah, thank you for great input during the editing process and much appreciation to the Create Space team for all your help moving VerAegis through the editing and publishing process.

Pastor Bill Heck, thank you for your sage counsel, patience, and passion, and for using your gift of teaching.

Pastors Bill Bucholtz of Family Community Church and Matt Hannon of New Heights Church, thank you for your passion and for using your God-given talents to teach.

Bruce Crawford, of Red Tail Woodworks, thank you for the inlay design of the sun and the photo of the three-legged stool.

Please note, those whom I acknowledge do not necessarily agree with all the concepts contained within *VerAegis*.

Bibliography

Aguilar, Franci J., and Arvind Bhambi. "Johnson and Johnson (A)." *Harvard Business School* 384–053: 1983.

Allen, David. Getting Things Done: The Art of Stress-Free Productivity. New York, New York: Penguin Books, 2002.

American Heart Association. "Overweight and Obesity (Statistical Fact Sheet, 2013 update)." Heart.org. 2013. Accessed January 2014. http://www.heart.org/idc/groups/heart-public/@wcm/@sop/@smd/documents/downloadable/ucm_319588.pdf.

Andretti, Mario, "Mario Andretti Quotes." Accessed 2015 http://www.brainyquote.com/quotes/quotes/m/marioandre130613.html

Angelou, Maya. "Maya Angelou Quotes." Accessed 2014 http://www.brainyquote.com/quotes/authors/m/maya_angelou.html.

Anthony, Marc. "Marc Anthony Quotes." Accessed 2013 http://www.brainyquote.com/quotes/authors/m/marc_anthony.html.

Aristotle. "Aristotle Qutoes." Accessed November 2013. http://www.brainyquote.com/quotes/authors/a/aristotle.html.

AutCom: Autism National Committee. "How to Think-and How Not to Think-About the Brain." Accessed November 2013. http://www.autcom.org/articles/HowToThink.html.

Bach, Richard. "Richard Bach Quotes." Accessed 2014 http://www.brainyquote.com/quotes/authors/r/richard_bach.html.

Bada, Jeffrey L., and Antonio Lazcano. "Stanley L. Miller 1930–2007; A Biographical Memoir." National Academy of Sciences on Line. 2012. Accessed 2014. http://www.nasonline.org/publications/biographical-memoirs/memoir-pdfs/miller-stanley.pdf.

Barton, Bruce. "Bruce Barton Quotes." Accessed 2014 http://www.brainyquote.com/quotes/authors/b/bruce_barton.html.

Beecher, Henry Ward. "Henry Ward Beecher Quotes." 2001–2013. Accessed October 2013. Henry Ward Beecher.

Bergland, Richard. The Fabric of the Mind. 1985. New York: Viking Penguin.

Berra, Yogi. "Yogi Berra Quotes." Accessed September 2013. http://www.brainyquote.com/quotes/.

Biblica. New International Version (NIV). Vers. New International Version. Biblica. Accessed 2013/2014. https://www.biblegateway.com/versions/New-International-Version-NIV-Bible/.

Bloom, Orlando. "Orlando Bloom Quotes." 2001–2013. Accessed October 2013. http://www.brainyquote.com/quotes/topics/topic_marriage2.html#cVScfz361pQlTmkQ.99.

Boa, Kenneth, and Larry Moody. I'm Glad You Asked. Wheaton, IL: Victor Books, SP Publications, 1982.

Bono, Edward de. "Six Thinking Hats." Accessed 2013 http://www.debonogroup.com/six_thinking_hats.php.

Boorstin, Daniel J. "Daniel J. Boorstin Quotes." 2001–2013. Accessed October 2013. http://www.brainyquote.com/quotes/quotes/d/danieljbo175243.html.

Bruyere, Jean de la. "Jean de la Bruyere Quote." Accessed 2014 http://www.brainyquote.com/quotes/quotes/j/jeandelabr402511.html.

Burns, John W., Phillip Quartana, Weley Gilliam, Erika Gray, Carla Nappi Justin Matsuura, Brandy Wolfe, and Kenneth Lofland. "Effects of anger suppression on pain severity and pain behaviors among chronic pain patients: Evaluation of an ironic process model." September 27, 2008. Accessed January 2014. http://psycnet.apa.org/journals/hea/27/5/645/.

Calcaterra, Nicholas Berne. "Transactional Analysis." 1999–2013. http://www.ericberne.com/transactional-analysis/.

Carnette, Jamal. "Investing Commentary: Here's Why Warren Buffett's Favorite Stock is Struggling." September 14, 2014. http://www.fool.com/investing/general/2014/09/14/heres-why-warren-buffetts-favorite-stock-is-strugg.aspx.

Carter, Dr. Les. The Anger Trap. San Francisco: Jossey-Bass, 2003.

Carter, Dr. Les, and Frank Minirth, M.D. The Anger Workbook. Nashville, Tennessee: Thomas Nelson, Inc., 1993.

The Case For Christ (Full Documentary). Directed by Lee Strobel, 2007.

CDC Office of the Associate Director for Communication, Digital Media Branch, Division of Public Affairs. "Insufficient Sleep Is a Public Health Epidemic." January 13, 2014. Accessed July 2014. http://www.cdc.gov/features/dssleep/.

Churchill, Winston. "Winston Churchill Quotes." Accessed October 2013. http://www.brainyquote.com/quotes/authors/w/winston_churchill.html.

"Coca-Cola: Our Company (Mission, Vison and Values)." Accessed 2014 http://www.coca-colacompany.com/our-company/mission-vision-values.

Collins, James C., and Jerry I. Porras. Built to Last. New York, New York: HarperCollins Publishers, Inc., 1994.

Collins, Jim. Good to Great. Harper Collins, 2001.

"Confronting the Unsustainable Growth of Welfare Entitlements." June, 2010. http://www.heritage.org/research/reports/2010/06/confronting-the-unsustainable-growth-of-welfare-entitlements-principles-of-reform-and-the-next-steps.

Covey, Steven R. "7 Habits of Highly Effective People Training Material."

———.The Seven Habits of Highly Effective People. New York, NY: Simon and Schuster, 1989.

Cox, Peter. "The Controversy of the Shack." June 19, 2009. Accessed October 11, 2013. http://www.examiner.com/article/the-controversy-of-the-shack.

Crick, Francis. Life Itself: Its Origin and Nature. London: Future, 1982.

Curatoloa, Gerry. "Carbohydrates." Accessed July 2014. http://www.sharecare.com/health/carbohydrates/sugar-consume-e -year

Damasio, Antonio. Descartes' Error: Emotion, Reason and the Human Brain. New York: Penguin, 1994.

de Bono, Edward. Lateral Thinking (Creativity Step by Step). New York, Philadelphia, St. Louis, San Francisco, London, Singapore, Sydney, Tokyo, Toronto: Harper & Row Publishers, 1970.

———. Six Thinking Hats. Boston, New York, London: Little, Brown and Company, 1985.

———. Six Thinking Hats. Boston, New York, London: Little, Bown and Company, 1999.

Derks, Eske M., James J. Hudziak, and Dorret I. Boomsma. "Why More Boys Than Girls with ADHD Recieve Treatment." Dutch Twin Register. Accessed 2014 http://www.tweelingenregister.org/publicaties/wetenschappelijke-publicaties/?no_cache=1&tx_sevenpack_pi1%5Bsearch%5D%5Brule%5D= AND&tx_sevenpack_pi1%5Bsearch%5D%5Bsep%5D=space&tx_sevenpack _pi1%5Byear%5D=2007&tx_sevenpack_pi1%5Bshow_uid%5D=160&cHash =79f1eee.

Dictionary.com. "Pharisees." Accessed March 2014. http://dictionary.reference.com/browse/Pharisees?s=t.

Drucker, Peter. "Peter Drucker Quotes." Accessed 2014 http://www.brainyquote.com/quotes/authors/p/peter_drucker.html.

Eastman, M.D., Mark, and Chuck Missler. "The Origin of Life and the Suppression of Truth." Accessed 2014. http://the_wordbride.tripod.com/origin.html.

Eastwood, Clint. "Clint Eastwood Quotes." Accessed 2013. http://www.brainyquote.com/quotes/authors/c/clint_eastwood.html

Edwards, Betty. The New Drawing on the Right Side of the Brain. Penguin Putnam Inc., 1999.

Eggerichs, Dr. Emerson. "Love and Respect Home Page." Accessed September 2013. http://loveandrespect.com/.

Eggerichs, Dr. Emerson. Love & Respect Small Group Discussion Guide. Grand Rapids: Love and Respect Ministries 2006.

Eisenhower, Dwight D. "Dwight D. Eisenhower Quotes" Accessed 2015 http://www.brainyquote.com/quotes/quotes/d/dwightdei149102.html

Einstein, Albert. "Albert Einstein Quotes." Accessed 2013. http://www.brainyquote.com/quotes/authors/a/albert_einstein_2.html.

Emerson, Ralph Waldo. "BrainyQuote." Accessed November 2013. http://www.brainyquote.com/quotes/authors/r/ralph_waldo_emerson.html.

"Emeth." Accessed October 2013. http://en.wikipedia.org/wiki/Emeth.

"Ephesians 2:10 (New International Version)." Accessed October 2013. http://www.biblegateway.com/passage/?search=Ephesians+2:10&version =NIV.

Epicurus. "Epicurus Quotes." Accessed January 2014. http://www.brainyquote.com/quotes/authors/e/epicurus.html.

"Face Illusions." Accessed 2013. http://brainden.com/optical-illusions.htm.

Ford, Henry. "Henry Ford Quotes." http://www.brainyquote.com/quotes/authors/h/henry_ford.html.

Fox News Insider. "Dr. Ben Carson Says Mayme White Miller Poem...Had Lasting Impact on Him." March 26, 2013. Accessed March 19, 2014. http://foxnewsinsider.com/2013/03/26/ben-carson-mother-poem-yourself-to-blame.

Franklin, Benjamin. "Benjamin Franklin Quotes." Accessed October 2013. http://www.brainyquote.com/quotes/authors/b/benjamin_franklin.html.

FranklinCovey. "FranklinCovey." Accessed 2014 http://www.franklincovey.com/tc/.

Gallistel, Charles R. The Organization of Learning (Learning, Development, and Conceptual Change). Cambridge: Bradford Books, 1993.

Gandhi, Mahatma. "Mahatma Gandhi Quotes." Accessed January 2014. http://www.brainyquote.com/quotes/authors/m/mahatma_gandhi.html.

"Genesis 2–3 (New International Version)." Accessed October 2013. http://www.biblegateway.com/passage/?search=Genesis%202&version= NIV.

Goethe, Johann Wolfgang von. Accessed January 2014 "Johann Wolfgang von Goethe Quotes." http://www.brainyquote.com/quotes/authors/j/johann_wolfgang_von_g oeth.html.

Goleman, Daniel. Accessed January 2014. "Daniel Goleman Quotes." http://www.brainyquote.com/quotes/authors/d/daniel_goleman.html.

Gordon, Authur. A Touch of Wonder. Fleming Revell Co., 1974.

Graham, Billy. "Billy Graham Quotes." Accessed January 2014. http://www.brainyquote.com/quotes/authors/b/billy_graham.html.

Grant, Amy. "Amy Grant Quotes." 2001–2013. Accessed October 2013. http://www.brainyquote.com/quotes/authors/a/amy_grant.html.

Green, Sir Philip. "Philip Green Quotes." Accessed 2014. http://www.brainyquote.com/quotes/authors/p/philip_green.html.

Greenleaf, Simon. "Testimony of the Evangelists." UMKC School of Law. 1846. Accessed June 2014. http://law2.umkc.edu/faculty/projects/ftrials/jesus/greenleaf.html.

Greenspan, Alan. "Alan Greenspan Quotes." Accessed December 2013. http://www.brainyquote.com/quotes/authors/a/alan_greenspan.html.

Hahn, Nhat. "Nhat Hahn Quotes." Accessed January 2014. "Nhat Hahn Quotes." http://www.brainyquote.com/quotes/authors/n/nhat_hanh.html.

Hamel, Gary. "Innovation's New Math Forget strategy sessions. To find one great idea, you must have workers dreaming up thousands." 2001. July 9. http://archive.fortune.com/magazines/fortune/fortune_archive/2001/07/09/306498/index.htm.

Hartman, Dr. Taylor. The People Code (Kindle Edition). New York, London, Toronto, Sydney: Scribner, 2007.

Helpern, Paul. "The Nature of Reality." October 10, 2012. http://www.pbs.org/wgbh/nova/blogs/physics/2012/10/how-large-is-the-observable-universe/.

Henley, Don, Michael Campbell, and John David Souther. "The Heart of The Matter Lyrics." http://www.lyricsfreak.com/d/don+henley/the+heart+of+the+matter_20042042.html.

Henry, Brad. "Brad Henry Quotes." Accessed December 2013. http://www.brainyquote.com/quotes/authors/b/brad_henry.html.

Hitler, Adolf. "Adolf Hitler Quotes." Accessed October 2013. http://www.brainyquote.com/quotes/authors/a/adolf_hitler.html.

Homer. "Homer Quotes." Accessed 2014. http://www.brainyquote.com/quotes/authors/h/homer.html.

Holzt, Lou. "Lou Holtz Quotes" Accessed 2015 http://www.brainyquote.com/quotes/quotes/l/louholtz450789.html

Houdmann, S. Michael. "Why did blood and water come out of Jesus' side when He was pierced?" Accessed June 2014. http://www.gotquestions.org/blood-water-Jesus.html#ixzz34wZyEuq7.

Hoyle, Sir Frederick. "Hoyle on Evolution." Nature 294 (1981): 105.

Hubbard, Elbert. "Elbert Hubbard Quotes." Accessed January 2014. http://www.brainyquote.com/quotes/authors/e/elbert_hubbard.html.

Ingram, Chip, and Dr. Becca Johnson. Overcoming Emotions That Destroy, ebook edition. Grand Rapids, MI: Baker Books, 2012.

"Innovation at Work." Innovation at Work. Audio Tech Business Book Summaries, 2001.

Jagger, Mick, and Keith Richards. "Rolling Stones Sympathy for the Devil Lyrics." Accessed October 2013. http://www.lyricsfreak.com/r/rolling+stones/sympathy+for+the+devil_20117881.html.

Jakes, T. D. Instinct: The Power to Unleash Your Inborn Drive. New York, Boston, Nashville: FaithWords, 2014.

James, Erwin. "'Dead Man' Talking." April 22, 2008. Accessed October 25, 2013. http://www.theguardian.com/society/2008/apr/23/prisonsandprobation.

James, William. The Principles of Psychology (Complete Vol. 1-2). 1890. Kindle Edition

Jastrow, Robert. God and the Astronomers. New York/London: W.W. Norton and Company, Inc., 1992.

Jefferson, Thomas. "Declaration of Independence." Accessed October 2013. http://www.archives.gov/exhibits/charters/declaration_transcript.html.

———. "Thomas Jefferson Quotes." Accessed October 2013. http://www.brainyquote.com/quotes/authors/t/thomas_jefferson.html.

Jerajani, H. R., Jaju Bhagyashri, M. M. Phiske, and Nitin Lade. Indian Journal of Dermatology. July–September 2009. http://www.ncbi.nlm.nih.gov/pmc/articles/PMC2810702/.

Johnson, Robert Wood. "Johnson&Johnson: Our Credo Values." 1943. http://www.jnj.com/about-jnj/jnj-credo/.

Jordan, Michael. "Michael Jordan Quotes." Accessed 2014. http://www.brainyquote.com/quotes/authors/m/michael_jordan.html.

Kahn, Jennifer. "Can Emotional Intelligence Be Taught." September 11, 2013. http://www.nytimes.com/2013/09/15/magazine/can-emotional-intelligence-be-taught.html?pagewanted=all&_r=2&.

Keats, Sharada, and Steve Wiggins. "Future Diets: Implications for Agriculutre and Food Prices." ODI.org. January 2014. http://www.odi.org/sites/odi.org.uk/files/odi-assets/publications-opinion-files/8776.pdf.

Keller, Helen. "Helen Keller Quotes." Accessed January 2014. http://www.brainyquote.com/quotes/authors/h/helen_keller.html.

Kelling, George L., and James Q. Willson. Broken Windows. March 1, 1982. Accessed March 19, 2014. http://www.theatlantic.com/magazine/archive/1982/03/broken-windows/304465/.

Kennedy, John F. "John F. Kennedy Quotes." Accessed January 2014. http://www.brainyquote.com/quotes/authors/j/john_f_kennedy.html.

Kiemele, Mark J., Stephen R. Schmidt, and Ronald J. Berdine. Basic Statistics Tools for Continuous Improvement Fourth Edition. Colorado Springs: Air Academy Press, LLC., 2000.

King, Martin Luther, Jr. "Martin Luther King, Jr. Quotes." Accessed December 2013. http://www.brainyquote.com/quotes/authors/m/martin_luther_king_jr.html.

Kipling, Rudyard. "Rudyard Kipling Quotes." Accessed December 2013. http://www.brainyquote.com/quotes/authors/r/rudyard_kipling.html.

Kittisak. "Golden Scales of Justice." Accessed 2014. http://www.freedigitalphotos.net/images/Other_Objects_g271-Golden_Scales_Of_Justice_p85202.html.

Klein, Gary. Sources of Power: How People Make Decisions. Cambridge, Massachusetts and London, England: MIT Press, 1998.

Klein, Sara. "Arenaline, Cortisol, Norepinephrine: The Three Major Stress Hormones, Explained." The Huffington Post. April 19, 2013.

http://www.huffingtonpost.com/2013/04/19/adrenaline-cortisol-stress-hormones_n_3112800.html.

Krakovsky, Marina. "How Do We Decide? Inside the 'Frinky' Science of the Mind." Winter 2010–11. Accessed November 2013. http://www.gsb.stanford.edu/news/bmag/sbsm0802/feature-babashiv.html.

Lehrer, Jonah. How We Decide. New York: First Mariner Books, 2009.

Lennox, Annie. "Annie Lennox Quotes." Accessed 2014 http://www.brainyquote.com/quotes/authors/a/annie_lennox.html.

Lewis, C. S. "C.S. Lewis Quotes." Accessed 2014 http://www.brainyquote.com/quotes/authors/c/c_s_lewis.html.

———. The Chronicles of Narnia: The Last Battle Chapter 15. London: Haper Collins, 1956.

———. The Collected Letters of C.S. Lewis, Volume 3. Kindle Edition. Harper Collins, 2009.

———. The Collected letters of C.S. Lewis, Volume III: Narnia. New York: Cambridge and Joy.

Lincoln, Abraham. "Abraham Lincoln Quotes." Accessed October 2013. http://www.brainyquote.com/quotes/authors/a/abraham_lincoln_2.html.

———. "The Gettysburg Address." November 19, 1863. Accessed October 2013. http://www.abrahamlincolnonline.org/lincoln/speeches/gettysburg.htm.

Lomong, Lopez, and Mark Tabb. Running For My Life. Nashville, Tennessee: Thomas Nelson, Inc., 2012.

Lowell, James Russell. "James Russell Lowell Quotes." Accessed 2014 http://www.brainyquote.com/quotes/authors/j/james_russell_lowell.html.

Maurois, Andre. "Andre Maurois Quotes." Accessed 2014 http://www.brainyquote.com/quotes/authors/a/andre_maurois.html.

Mayo Clinic Staff. "Adult Health: Anger management: 10 tips to tame your temper." Accessed 2014 http://www.mayoclinic.com/health/anger-management/MH00102.

McCall, Ash. "A Timeline of Operation Desert Storm." February 26, 2013. Accessed November 2013. http://armylive.dodlive.mil/index.php/2013/02/operation-desert-storm/.

Meeker, Meg, M.D. Strong Fathers, Strong Daughters 10 Secrets Every Father Should Know. Washington, DC: Regnery Publishing, Inc., 2006.

Moore, Billy. "Billy Moore: People in prison can change." Accessed October 2013. http://www.nodeathpenalty.org/new_abolitionist/february-2005-issue-34/billy-moore-people-prison-can-change.

"MSN Money: Bristol-Myers Squibb Com (NYSE:BMY)." September 16, 2014. http://investing.money.msn.com/investments/charts?symbol=US:BMY#{"zRange":"10","startDate":"1900-1-1","endDate":"2014-9-

24","chartStyle":"mountain","chartCursor":"1","scaleType":"0","yaxisAlign
":"right","mode":"pan"}.

"MSN Money: Johnson and Johnson (NYSE: JNJ)." September 16, 2014.
http://investing.money.msn.com/investments/charts?symbol=US:JNJ#{"zR
ange":"10","startDate":"1972-6-30","endDate":"2014-9-
15","chartStyle":"mountain","chartCursor":"1","scaleType":"0","yaxisAlign
":"right","mode":"pan"}.

Nicks, Denver. "Study: Obesity Rates Have Surged in the Developming World."
January 03, 2014. Accessed January 2014.
http://healthland.time.com/2014/01/03/study-obesity-rates-have-surged-
in-developing-world/.

Niebuhr, Reinhold. "Reinhold Niebuhr Quotes." Accessed 2014
http://www.brainyquote.com/quotes/authors/r/reinhold_niebuhr.html.

Norton, Roger J. "'s Invitation to Speak at Gettysburg and the Meaning of the
Gettysburg Address." Accessed 2013.
http://rogerjnorton.com/Lincoln58.html.

Nosowitz, Dan. "The Big Bang May not Have Spawned the Universe After All."
September 18, 2013. Accessed April 2014.
http://www.popsci.com/science/article/2013-09/big-bang-may-not-have-
spawned-universe-after-all.

Orman, Suze. "Suze Orman Quotes." Accessed December 2013.
http://www.brainyquote.com/quotes/authors/s/suze_orman.html.

Osteen, Joel. "Joel Osteen Quotes." Accessed 2014
http://www.brainyquote.com/quotes/authors/j/joel_osteen.html.

Oz, Mehmet, MD. "Carbohydrates." Accessed July 2014.
http://www.sharecare.com/health/carbohydrates/sugar-consume-every-
year.

Peet, J. H. "The Miller-Urey Experiment." Accessed 2014.
http://www.truthinscience.org.uk/tis2/index.php/evidence-for-evolution-
mainmenu-65/51-the-miller-urey-experiment.html.

Pippert, Rebecca. Hope has its Reasons. Harper, 1990.

"Politics and City Life: Chicago." September 21, 2012.
http://www.chicagomag.com/Chicago-Magazine/October-2012/Chicago-
Tylenol-Murders-An-Oral-History/.

Reagan, Ronald. "Ronald Reagan Quotes." Accessed October 2013.
http://www.brainyquote.com/quotes/authors/r/ronald_reagan.html.

Renner, Kevin. In Search of Fatherhood: Stories from Women Around the World,
Kindle Edition. Publish Your Words, 2011.

Reuther, Walter. "Walter Reuther Quotes." Accessed 2014
http://www.brainyquote.com/quotes/authors/w/walter_reuther.html.

Richardson, Renelle. "The 700 Club." Accessed 2014
http://www.cbn.com/700club/features/amazing/billy_moore040209.aspx
.

Robbins, Tony. "Tony Robbins Quotes." Accessed 2014 http://www.brainyquote.com/quotes/authors/t/tony_robbins.html.

Rogers, Will. "Will Rogers Quotes." Accessed December 2013. http://www.brainyquote.com/quotes/authors/w/will_rogers.html.

Rohn, Jim. "Jim Rohn Quotes." Accessed 2014 http://www.brainyquote.com/quotes/authors/j/jim_rohn.html.

Roosevelt, Eleanor. "Eleanor Roosevelt Quotes." Accessed 2014 http://www.brainyquote.com/quotes/authors/e/eleanor_roosevelt.html.

Roosevelt, Theodore. "Theodore Roosevelt Quotes." Accessed October 2013. http://www.brainyquote.com/quotes/authors/t/theodore_roosevelt.html

Rothermel, Richard C. "US Forest Service: Rocky Mountain Research Station." TreeSearch. May 1993. Accessed November 2013. http://www.treesearch.fs.fed.us/pubs/viewpub.jsp?index=4613.

Rudner, Rita. "Rita Rudner Quotes.". Accessed October 2013. http://www.brainyquote.com/quotes/authors/r/rita_rudner.html.

SavannahNow. "Arthur Gordon (1912–2002)." January 5, 2002. Accessed 2014 http://savannahnow.com/stories/010502/LOCgordonobit.shtml.

Saxenain, Hrand. "Maturity in Motion; Design for Leadership." Accessed 2014 http://h2notes.org/maturityinmotion.html.

Schultz, Bob. Boyhood and Beyond, Practical Wisdom for Becoming a Man. Eugene, OR: Great Expectations Book Company, 2004.

Schweitzer, Albert. "Albert Schweitzer Quotes." Accessed 2014 http://www.brainyquote.com/quotes/authors/a/albert_schweitzer.html.

Scully, Vin. "Vin Scully Quotes." Accessed October 2013. http://www.brainyquote.com/quotes/authors/v/vin_scully.html.

Seneca, Lucius Annaeus. "Lucius Annaeus Seneca Quotes." Accessed 2013 http://www .brainyquote.com/quotes/authors/l/lucius_annaeus_seneca.html.

Smith, Barbara. "Barbara Smith Quotes." Accessed 2014 http://www.brainyquote.com/quotes/authors/b/barbara_smith.html.

Solzhenitsyn, Aleksandr. "Aleksandr Solzhenitsyn Quotes." Accessed November 2013. http://www.brainyquote.com/quotes/authors/a/ aleksandr_solzhenitsyn. html.

Spool, Jared M. "The KJ-Technique: A Group Process for Establishing Priorities." May 11, 2004. http://www.uie.com/articles/kj_technique/.

Staff Reports. "Rome News-Tribune." February 19, 2012. Accessed November 2012. http://cc.bingj.com/cache.aspx?q=Is+Billy+Moore+The+only+confessed+murderer+paroled+from+death+row&d=4948688248309041&mkt=en-US&setlang=en-US&w=Z7UHXv3Ox27KZy_Lzw3_JuOYtkcN4B1h.

Stalin, Joseph. "Joseph Stalin Quotes." Accessed October 2013. p://www.brainyquote.com/quotes/authors/j/joseph_stalin.html.

Stanton, Glenn T. "First-Person: The Christian Divorce Rate Myth." February 15, 2011. http://www.bpnews.net/BPnews.asp?ID=34656.

"Steven R. Covey Quotes." Accessed September 7, 2013. http://www.great-quotes.com/quotes/author/Stephen+R./Covey.

Stevenson, Mary. "Footprints in the Sand." Accessed December 2013. http://www.footprints-inthe-sand.com/index.php?page=Poem/Poem.php.

Stork, Dr. Travis. "The Effects of Suppressing Anger." November 9, 2012. Accessed 2014 http://on.aol.com/video/the-effects-of-suppressing-anger-517534016.

Storm, Howard. "Atheist College Professor Dies and Sees Hell and Demons--it changed his life." December 13, 2011. https://www.youtube.com/watch?v=kLimoqZUWgw.

Strickland, Jonathan. "How the Big Bang Theory Works." Accessed 2014. http://science.howstuffworks.com/dictionary/astronomy-terms/big-bang-theory7.htm.

Stump, Mr. B. "Phineas Gage Didactic 2 Part Series." Accessed November 2013. http://www.youtube.com/watch?v=5nr06A3cHQA.

Suzy Platt Congressional Research Service. Respectfully Quoted: A Dictionary of Quotations from the Library of Congress. Edited by Suzy Platt. Washington DC: Congressional Quarterly Inc., 1992.

Tada, Joni Eareckson. "Joni Eareckson Tada Quotes." Accessed February 2014. http://www.brainyquote.com/quotes/authors/j/joni_eareckson_tada.html.

———. "Larry King Show-Joni Eareckson Tada Story." June 06, 2009. http://www.youtube.com/watch?v=Foffh-gneRs.

Tannenbaum Center for Interreligious Understanding. "The Golden Rule." Accessed October 2013. https://www.tanenbaum.org/resources/golden-rule?gclid=CLqG85mbnroCFUFxQgodp0sAkA.

Thatcher, Margaret. "Margaret Thatcher Quotes." Accessed 2014. http://www.brainyquote.com/quotes/authors/m/margaret_thatcher.html

The Case for a Creator. Grand Rapids, Michigan: Zondervan, 2004.

The Case for Christ--A Journalist's Personal Investigation of the Evidence for Jesus. Grand Rapids, Michigan: Zonderland Publishing House, 1998.

The Case for Faith. Grand Rapids, Michigan: Zonderan, 2000.

The Case for a Creator: A Six-Session Investigation of the Scientific Evidence that Points Toward God. Directed by Lee Strobel and Garry Poole. 2008.

The Lockman Foundation. "New American Standard Bible (NASB). Vers. New American Standard Bible." Accessed 2013–2014. https://www.biblegateway.com/versions/New-American-Standard-Bible-NASB.

Thomas Nelson, Inc. "New King James Version (NKJV). Vers. New King James Version." Accessed 2013–2014. https://www.biblegateway.com.

Thoreau, Henry David. "Henry David Thoreau Quotes." Accessed November 2013. http://www.brainyquote.com/quotes/authors/h/henry_david_thoreau.html.

Todd, Jody. "Practical Applications for Husbands and Wives." March 22, 2010. Accessed September 2013. http://unraveled1207.wordpress.com/category/online-studies/love-respect-online-study/.

Townsend. Aesop's Fables (Kindle Edition). Amazon Digital Services, Inc.

Tracy, Brian. "Brian Tracy Quotes." Accessed January 2014. http://www.brainyquote.com/quotes/authors/b/brian_tracy.html.

Tung, Mao Tse. "150 Quotes from Mao Tse Tung." Accessed October 2013. http://www.marxists.org/reference/archive/mao/works/red-book/quotes.htm.

———. "Mao Zedong Quotes." Accessed October 2013. http://www.brainyquote.com/quotes/authors/m/mao_zedong.html.

Twain, Mark. "Mark Twain Quotes." Accessed 2013. http://www.brainyquote.com/quotes/authors/m/mark_twain.html.

Tyndale House Foundation. "New Living Translation (NLT)." Accessed 2013. https://www.biblegateway.com/versions/New-Living-Translation-NLT-Bible/.

Varun, Porwal (Bryan Dyson). "30 Second Speech By Bryan Dyson (Former CEO of Coca-Cola)." 2011. http://inspirationaldaily.wordpress.com/2011/12/22/30-second-speech-by-bryan-dyson-former-ceo-of-coca-cola/.

Viorst, Judith. "Judith Viorst Quotes." Accessed March 2014. http://www.brainyquote.com/quotes/authors/j/judith_viorst.html.

Wadsworth, Walter J. "Goal Setting and Achievement." Bristol Vermont: Velocity Business Publishing, 1997.

Waitley, Denis. "Denis Waitley Quotes." Accessed 2014 http://www.brainyquote.com/quotes/authors/d/denis_waitley.html.

Warren, Rick. The Purpose Driven Life. Grand Rapids: Zondervan, 2002.

Wiggins, Steve; Keats, Sharada. "Future Diets: Implications for agricultural and food prices." ODI.org.uk. January 2014. Accessed January 2014. http://www.odi.org.uk/sites/odi.org.uk/files/odi-assets/publications-opinion-files/8776.pdf.

Wikipedia. "W. Edwards Deming." Accessed October 2013. http://en.wikipedia.org/wiki/W._Edwards_Deming.

Wiley, Josh. "22 Awesome C.S. Lewis Quotes." October 23, 2011. Accessed September 4, 2013. http://www.whatchristianswanttoknow.com/22-awesome-c-s-lewis-quotes/.

Winfrey, Oprah. "Oprah Winfrey Quotes." Accessed March 2014. http://www.brainyquote.com/quotes/authors/o/oprah_winfrey.html.

Young, William P. The Shack. Los Angeles: windblown Media, 2007.

Ziglar, Zig. "Zig Ziglar Quotes." Accessed 2104 http://www.brainyquote.com/quotes/authors/z/zig_ziglar.html.